I Hate Witnessing

A HANDBOOK FOR EFFECTIVE CHRISTIAN COMMUNICATION

DICK INNES

Scripture quotations in this publication are from the *New International Version,* Holy Bible. Copyright 1973 and 1978 by New York International Bible Society. Used by permission.

Also quoted are:

TLB—The Living Bible, Copyright 1971 by Tyndale House Publishers, Wheaton, Illinois. Used by permission.

Phillips—The New Testament in Modern English, Revised Edition, J.B. Phillips, Translator. © J.B. Phillips 1958, 1960, 1972. Used by permission of Macmillan Publishing Company, Inc.

KJV—The Authorized King James Version

Published by Vision House Inc.

A Division of GL Publications
Ventura, California 93006
Printed in U.S.A.

Library of Congress Cataloging in Publication Data

Innes, Dick.
    I hate witnessing.

    Includes bibliographical references.
    I. Witness bearing (Christianity)   I. Title.
BV4520.I45   1983   248'.5   83-10246
ISBN 0-88449-106-4

Contents

Prologue

Acknowledgements

One person could never take all the credit for that which he writes or teaches. All of us are the sum total of our past experiences and the influences others have had upon us. Thus it wouldn't be possible to thank the many people who have contributed to the writing of this book. However, I would like to mention just a few. Thanks to Muriel, my wife, who has led me to an understanding of people's needs more than anyone else; to Jim Engle for imparting to me an invaluable understanding of communication theory; to Glenn Arnold whose "show me—don't tell me" philosophy of writing gave me a simple but profound key for communicating any message; to Terri Knorr for typing and retyping this manuscript; to Carol Lacy for polishing this manuscript and encouraging me to keep on writing; to my supporting churches and individuals and to my board and staff who have shared in and made my ministry for Christ possible; and most of all to God for the opportunity to share a message which I trust might be used of Him to influence others as I myself have been influenced by so many others.

Dick Innes
Claremont, California

I HATE WITNESSING

"This book should be read by every Christian, not only to relieve forever the false guilt about witnessing, but in order to learn how to become better communicators and more loving, accepting persons. It is spiritually and psychologically stimulating. Dick Innes is a great communicator."

Cecil G. Osborne
Author of the best-seller—
THE ART OF UNDERSTANDING YOUR-SELF

PROLOGUE

It was a beautiful morning. The sky was a brilliant blue. Bathers were already soaking up the sunshine and challenging the surf. Only the edges of the sea seemed ruffled as its waves thundered down on the beach. But the great expanse of the Pacific, living up to its name, seemed to stand idly by with nothing to do except reflect the brilliant blue of the sky.

High above, I sat on my private balcony at the Waikiki Beach Holiday Inn, soaking up the magnificent view. I was in Hawaii on a brief stopover while crossing the Pacific. Now I was having my morning devotions. That day I wanted to tell God something that had been bothering me for a long time.

I had spent several years training for Christian work. I had pastored a church and was now the director of a Christian organization whose work was evangelism. But I had a big problem and needed to tell God about it.

"God," I nervously prayed, "I know that as a Christian and especially as a Christian minister I'm supposed to be doing a lot of witnessing for you. I know that I should be sharing your plan of salvation more than I am. Furthermore, it's my job. But, God, I'm sick to death of witnessing for you out of a sense of duty and trying to tell others about you because that's what I'm supposed to do. In spite of all my years of training and experience, I am as frightened as ever to witness. I have never found it easy. I hate witnessing and I'm quitting! I absolutely refuse to keep playing this game any longer. I'm afraid I'm finished."

I waited for the lightning to strike—but nothing happened.

I'm not a mystic. I'd never seen any great visions or heard God speak to me in any dramatic ways before, but that morning I felt I heard God speak to me. Deep inside I heard His still small voice, "Amen, Dick, I hate the way you witness too."

The kind of witnessing I hated was sharing the gospel more out of a sense of guilt and compulsion rather than out of a sense of freedom and liberty. It's that little voice inside your head that keeps on saying, "You've got to do it!" And when you do, you're so uptight you feel you'd burst if somebody stuck a pin in you.

It's like the minister who said, "I feel guilty when I don't witness to my neighbors. And I feel guilty when I do because I make such a botch of it. My approach is so unnatural."

I like the way Rebecca Pippert describes her feelings about this kind of witnessing. She writes, "There was a part of me that secretly felt evangelism was something you shouldn't do to your dog, let alone a friend . . . . Still, I knew that Christians were called on to do hard things. And because it was so hard to do I thought such evangelism had to be spiritual. The result was that I would put off witnessing as long as possible. Whenever the guilt became too great to bear, I overpowered the nearest non-Christian with a nonstop running monolog and then dashed away thinking, 'Whew! Well, I did it. It's spring of '74 and hopefully the guilt won't overcome me again 'til winter of '75.' (And my non-Christian friends hoped the same!)

"I witnessed like a Pavlovian dog. The bell would ring, I would get ready, activated, juices running and them BAM! I'd spit it out."[1]

Many readers will readily identify with this type of witnessing experience. How often we've tried, but failed miserably. Perhaps the secret in successfully presenting the gospel lies in learning to differentiate between what we have come to think of as witnessing and what Jesus actually meant in Acts 1:8. I believe it does.

It's one thing to witness. It can be altogether another thing to communicate to someone else what Jesus wanted "Jerusalem, and . . . Judea and Samaria, and . . . the ends of the earth" to know. The intent of this book is not to discourage those who have the God-given gift of personal evangelism but to help the 99 percent who don't have this gift to better understand what Jesus meant about witnessing.

Be Honest
I grew up in a conservative church. From my youth I have been taught the importance of witnessing for Christ. I'm not sure that my church knew how to do it, but it did teach that "the supreme task of the church is the evangelization of the world."

I believed it then. I believe it now.

I'm certain that most Christians believe this too and take Christ's last command seriously. You are to "go into all the world and preach the good news to all creation," He said to His followers immediately before returning to heaven (Mark 16:15).

But how many of us, if we will be truly honest, actually enjoy witnessing for Christ? How many find it easy? How many love to do it? How many have tried but were always scared? How many have learned witnessing methods or became involved in witnessing programs, tried them for a while, but felt as if they were having to force themselves to do it? And how many have quit witnessing altogether because they became too discouraged?

And how many still feel they ought to be witnessing more for Christ but feel guilty because they're not?

If you feel this way, you're not alone. Time and again I have asked church congregations how many really love to witness for Christ. Very few respond in the affirmative. But when I ask how many, like me, are afraid to witness, find it difficult, and don't like doing it, almost everyone quietly slips up his or her hand.

One can almost feel a great sigh of relief among the people when they discover that they are not alone in their struggle—and even many Christian workers and ministers, like me, feel the same way.

> Even among Christ's disciples only one had the gift of personal evangelism.

Occasionally one finds some who enjoy sharing their Christian faith. They do it naturally and with ease. They have a real gift in this area. However, most of us don't. Even among Christ's twelve disciples, probably only one had the gift of personal evangelism. It was Andrew. He was the one who introduced Peter to Jesus. He was the one who found the boy with the loaves and fish and brought him to Jesus. And he was the one who introduced the Greek inquirers to Jesus.

Therefore, you shouldn't be worried if you don't have the gift of personal evangelism. Like the rest of the disciples, you can learn effective ways to communicate Christ's message without getting uptight about it, and in the process come to appreciate it and have your own life greatly enriched as a result.

The first requirement is to be honest about your feelings. If you find witnessing difficult and hate doing it, admit it. Tell a friend. Tell God. He knows it anyhow. As long as you deny your true feelings, you will act them out blindly in self-defeating ways. Only as you admit what you truly feel, can God help you.

Be Available
The next requirement is simply to make yourself available for God to use. Going back to my prayer at Honolulu, after I told God that I hated witnessing and was going to quit, I continued with my prayer.

"However, God," I said, "even though I hate witnessing, if you want to use me to bring your message of love and salvation to others, then I'm available. But you'll have to do it through me as I'm just too scared to do it myself."

My witnessing life for Christ has never been the same since. That was one of the most honest prayers I had ever prayed. It changed my life.

Within a few hours I resumed my journey. I was in a jumbo jet that had very few passengers. I was sitting in a row of seats all by myself, reading a book about the return of Christ which a friend had given to me.

Most of the seats ahead of me were empty except for one. There sat a lone man. At one point he got up and came back and sat beside me. He introduced himself to me and I introduced myself to him.

"What's the book you're reading?" he inquired.

"It's a book about the second coming of Christ," I replied.

"Do you believe that Christ is coming to earth again?" he asked sincerely.

"Yes, I do," I admitted, not knowing what to expect next.

"That's interesting," he said. "Will you please tell me all about it?"

I couldn't help myself. Instead of my buttonholing him and trying to force the Christian message on him, he literally drew it out of me.

I love witnessing like that! And all I had done was tell God that I was available if He wanted to use me. A similar thing happened on the next flight I was on.

The exact same thing hasn't happened since, but I believe God used those particular experiences as a confirmation that my confession to Him was honest, that He had heard my prayer and that I was getting on the right track. However, since that time God has led me into a communication ministry that is bringing the Christian message to many people in terms they can understand and appreciate, and in ways that are rewarding to me. The secret has been in being honest with my feelings, being available to God to use, and learning to communicate and not merely witness. So while I hate witnessing in the sense we've been talking about, I do love to communicate.

Note

1. Rebecca Manley Pippert, *Out of the Saltshaker and into the World* (Downers Grove, IL: Inter-Varsity Press, 1979), pp. 15-17.

Part I
Quit "Witnessing"

One

GETTING OFF THE GUILT TRIP

How do you feel when you are driving along the highway and a police car pulls alongside you?

If you're like me, you probably feel your stomach tighten, you automatically go for the brake, quickly check your speed, and sigh with relief when you see that you aren't going over the speed limit.

You weren't breaking the law, so why did you feel guilty? Mostly because of false guilt. When your guard was down, the sudden appearance of the policeman triggered this guilt. Had it been a common practice for you to go over the speed limit it probably would have triggered real guilt as well.

Guilt and its close ally *legalism* are used rather extensively in modern society as motivators—especially guilt. They get quick results, but are never lasting. They also damage people psychologically, and are two of the most commonly used but worst motivators for getting people to witness for Christ.

To become an effective Christian communicator, one needs to be freed from these false motivators. In the long run they are destructive and self-defeating. Only as one is freed from a "having-to-do-it" motive can he become free to "want to do it."

Freedom from Guilt

Whether a person's guilt is true or false, it has the same negative effect when used as a motivator. True guilt is a result of having done something you know to be wrong. It is resolved when confession and restitution are made. False guilt is much harder to resolve for the simple fact that it isn't guilt. It is very often a result of parental (or parental type) programming which has been used as a means of controlling one's children. It is always accompanied with conditional love. In other words, if the child conformed to the parent's every wish he was given love and affection. If he didn't conform, the parents withdrew their love and had a subtle way of making the child feel guilty. Like with Pavlov's dogs, the false guilt became an unconscious conditioned response.

> "False guilt comes as a result of the judgments and suggestions of men."

Paul Tournier, the eminent Christian therapist, distinguishes between the two guilts as follows: "False guilt is that which comes as a result of the judgments and suggestions of men. True guilt is that which results from divine judgment."[1]

Unfortunately, there are many Christians who have an overload of false guilt. Whenever things go wrong they feel responsible. They feel that they are to blame whether they are or not. That little voice inside their head keeps saying, "You're guilty." These people are sincere. They truly want to serve Christ and His church, but if we ministers and leaders aren't careful, we can readily tap into their feelings of guilt and get them to do just about anything we want them to do, but with poor results.

According to Em Griffin, author of the book *The Mind Changers*, "Research shows that guilt is a powerful tool to get people to do what they wouldn't do normally. Before we rush off to use guilt as a technique to win people to Jesus Christ [or try to motivate others to win people to Christ], we need to see the long-term effects of the tactic. As it turns out, persuasion through guilt has some potent side effects which can harm the cause of Christ."[2]

Griffin goes on to say that guilt causes avoidance, devaluates, and obtains only outward conformity. Guilt also can be used to control people, to unconsciously drive people to make amends, and cause compulsive behavior.

Causes avoidance. If you have stolen my lawn mower, every time you see me, you're going to feel your guilt and will avoid any close contact with me.

False guilt has the same effect. If I'm the kind of leader or speaker who constantly makes you feel guilty, you will still tend to withdraw from and avoid me.

Devaluates. Furthermore, if I make you feel guilty you will not like me and will lose respect for me. "This is similar to what police discover in criminal investigations. After the crime, the guilty party sees the victim as having little worth. As ambassadors for Jesus Christ, our aim is to encourage people to love and worship our Lord. Making them feel guilty toward him produces the exact opposite result."[3]

Obtains outward conformity. The local Freedom from Hunger Committee may make you feel guilty to get you to help them collect or raise funds. You may conform outwardly because you feel obliged to help, but feel angry inside because you didn't want to. Thus there will be no internal or long-term commitment to their cause—as valid as it is.

Using guilt to motivate people to serve Christ and spread the gospel can and does damage a person's long-term commitment to Christ and the church. It makes people angry or depressed and drives them away from good causes—including the Great Commission.

Controls people. Sad to say, we have too often used guilt in the church to control and "motivate" people. When they conform to the spoken or unspoken rules and expectations they are given warmth, acceptance, and approval. However, when a person doesn't conform to those expectations he is readily made to feel guilty and experience rejection. All too often many of these expectations are cultural rather than biblical.

> When I used guilt as a motivator, the "guilty" ones responded—that is, those with an overload of false guilt.

As a young and inexperienced pastor I sometimes was guilty (unconsciously) of using guilt as a motivator. I had a strong desire to see my church grow and have the people out witnessing for Christ in the neighborhood. Not that there was anything wrong with this goal. There wasn't. It was how I handled it that was at fault. By overemphasizing the need to get out and witness, and by quoting the "appropriate" Scriptures, I made many of the people feel guilty. The problem was that when I used guilt as the motivator, the "guilty" ones responded; that is, those with an overload of false guilt. Often the ones who weren't equipped to do visitation were the ones who came out to help, while other "guilty" ones withdrew from and mostly avoided witnessing altogether.

Using a false motivator, I now question my own motives in wanting my people to go out and witness. Was I more concerned about winning the lost or with building a bigger, more successful church? I'm sure it was a mixture of both and the latter may very well have been the predominant factor.

Drives people to make amends. Unresolved guilt, either true or false, can drive people unconsciously to do good works, including witnessing. It is a problem none of us is immune from. This guilt, which gives a feeling of being unclean or unworthy, "creates a need to make amends, to make restitution, to suffer enough to pay back what is amiss, to set things 'right.' . . . It is not merely a problem with a few extreme masochists (those who gain neurotic pleasure from their own pain), but it is very much a factor in every person."[4]

Causes inner compulsions. If an individual is being motivated to witness for Christ out of a sense of guilt, he needs to carefully examine his motivation. "Where the Spirit of the Lord is, there is freedom" (2 Cor. 3:17); that is, a spirit of freedom.

> If a person is controlled by guilt, he is not being controlled by the Holy Spirit.

If one is being driven to witness out of a sense of inner compulsion and not out of a spirit of freedom, he is not being led by the Spirit of God but rather by his own guilt. To put it another way, if a person is being motivated and controlled by guilt, he is not being motivated and controlled by the Holy Spirit— no matter how strong the feelings are that tell him he should be witnessing. Compulsions are never of God. They are actually neurotic symptoms caused by unresolved inner problems and "give a mighty foothold to the devil" (Eph. 4:27, *TLB*) to really foul us up in our thinking.

To find the freedom of Christ, one must of necessity see through and get off his guilt trip, which may very well mean that he will need to stop witnessing altogether for a time until he resolves his guilt and is freed to share his Christian faith out of a spirit of freedom and love.

The point is this, you don't *have* to go out and witness for Christ. God wants you to be free from this bondage and guilt that says you *have* to. He wants you just *to be* His witness before you go out and *do* anything. And once you know at the feeling level that you don't have to witness, something very interesting happens, you are freed to want to do it. It is such a liberating experience when one realizes that his compulsions come from within himself and not from God.

Em Griffin tells an ironic story about a boy who wouldn't eat his prunes at dinner. "His mother made the ultimate threat: 'God won't like it if you don't eat them,' she declared. Yet he continued to sit stubbornly, so she sent him to his room. Later there was a severe thunderstorm. His mother tiptoed into the room to soothe him so he wouldn't be scared. But as it turned out he was sitting by the window watching the lightning play across the sky with an amused expression on his face. As she drew near, she overheard him say to himself, 'Tch, tch! Such a fuss over a few lousy prunes.' In this case the boy accepted his mother's judgment of guilt but ended up viewing God as slightly ridiculous. Perhaps conviction of sin is best left to the Holy Spirit."[5]

Conviction for Christian obedience, including witnessing for Christ, is also best left to the Holy Spirit. If I motivate you to witness out of guilt, or you feel that you have to witness for Christ out of a sense of guilt, we're both heading for trouble. We both may see short-term results and be tempted to believe our actions are of God. However, the long-term results are bound to be damaging. As the Apostle Paul put it, "Godly sorrow brings repentance that leads to salvation and leaves no regret, but worldly sorrow brings death" (2 Cor. 7:10).

Freedom from Legalism

Like false guilt, legalism too has some pretty potent side effects.

Jim Smith, a friend of mine, grew up in a fairly legalistic environment. He was taught that to be a good Christian he must be constantly telling others about God's plan of salvation. He admitted to me that whenever he traveled on public transport he was so scared that he would have to talk about Christ to the person sitting beside him that he always tried to sit next to an empty seat. I'm sure that many of us can identify with those feelings. I certainly can.

Bruce Larson, Christian author, talks about his legalistic programming and how difficult it is to overcome. He writes, "One of my own early spiritual heroes taught me that 'unless one is winning (converts), one is sinning.' And conversely, that 'when one is sinning, one cannot be winning.' In other words, I would be leading people to Christ regularly

"SO THIS IS WHAT I GET FOR HITTING MY SIS-TER."

and frequently if I were truly in the will of God. I still find myself at times straining in relationships to 'win someone.' It is hard to overcome those deep-rooted feelings that 'winning' marks my own authenticity as a Christian."[6]

Legalism is also a poor motivator and has some very negative effects. It keeps people in bondage. It damages people psychologically because it keeps them overdependent and immature. And it kills the soul. One difference between guilt and legalism is that guilt is a false internal motivator, while legalism is a false external motivator. However, they work together and, like overdependency and alcoholism, they feed on each other.

Legalism is lethal. Christian duty when practiced for the right motive is creative. When it becomes legalistic it kills the soul. As far back as 1645 Samuel Bolton wrote that "the Godly man goes to duty as a means of communion with God, to see God, to enjoy God, and to talk to God; the other goes to duty merely to satisfy the grumblings and quarrels of his conscience."[7]

According to the Apostle Paul, following the external letter of the law kills. He wrote, "We deal not in the letter but in the Spirit. The letter of the Law leads to the death of the soul; the Spirit of God alone can give life to the soul" (2 Cor. 3:6, *Phillips*).

Legalism keeps people in bondage. Obviously a society or group cannot operate without rules. If everybody did his own thing on the highway, there would be mass slaughter. The rules of the road are to keep people safe and get them to where they are going. That's the whole purpose of the law. However, rules can be used not only to save people but to enslave them. If a government uses its laws to control people and use people for its own purposes, that people is enslaved. History will readily verify this.

Richard J. Foster talks about the Christian disciplines, of which witnessing for Christ is one, and says that when they "degenerate into law, they are used to manipulate and control people. We take explicit commands and use them to imprison others. The result of such deterioration of the spiritual disciplines is pride and fear. Pride takes over because we come to believe that we are the right kind of people. Fear takes over because the power of controlling others carries with it the anxiety of losing control, and the anxiety of being controlled by others."[8]

Legalism is sinful. The legalistic, controlling person is an insecure person who feels safe only when he has everything under his control. Whether this over-control is done in the name of child rearing or religion, it is equally damaging to human personality because it stops people growing. We tend to think of sin as performing certain acts or of breaking certain rules. But sin is not merely adhering to a list of dos and don'ts. Sin is anything that damages people or hinders their maturity. An action is not wrong because the Bible says so; the Bible says it's wrong because it is harmful to human personality. Therefore, because legalism is so damaging to human personality, it is sinful.

Legalism is satanic. In fact, Paul took it a step further. He stated emphatically that legalism was of the devil. The Galatian Christians were beginning to slip away from their freedom in Christ back into legalism which prompted Paul to ask them, "Who has bewitched [or bedeviled] you?" (Gal. 3:1).

Those of us who work with people and see the effects of legalism know that it is a curse. Psychiatric clinics also testify to this fact. Their couches are filled with people whose personalities have been badly damaged as a result of having grown up under too legalistic a rod. There was absolutely nobody that Jesus condemned as He did the Pharisees because of their self-righteous legalism.

Legalism is pharisaical. The Pharisees had rules and regulations for all aspects of life, but their relationships with the common people were about zero. Their strict adherence to rules actually kept them apart from people. On the outside they appeared to be almost perfect, but on the inside they were very rigid. Their legalism or theological rigidity was not a sign of spirituality but a symptom of emotional rigidity and was a basic defense against facing their inner insecurities. Sad to say, some religious groups still believe that theological rigidity is a sign of spirituality when, in fact, it is a sign of emotional rigidity, immaturity, and insecurity.

> Jesus always spoke with authority, but He was never authoritarian.

Legalism is authoritarian but it has no real authority—only control. Unlike Jesus, the Pharisees were authoritarian but had no authority because their motives were all wrong. Their legalism was an external cover of inner fear—an outward show of strength as an overcompensation for their inner weakness. In direct contrast, Jesus always spoke with authority, but He was never authoritarian. He was real. He was secure. He didn't have a need to control people. He loved them. As Carl Jung said, "Where there is love, there is no will to power" or control. To be led by a legalist is never to be led by the Lord, because the Lord was never legalistic.

Finally, legalism destroys relationships. Rules make people feel safe. There are no risks involved. The answers are all predetermined—by someone else. There is less chance of making mistakes or of getting hurt. People don't have to think for themselves, determine what is right or wrong for themselves, or trust God for themselves. It is all done for them. But they are kept over-dependent and immature. Furthermore, hiding behind rules, they don't open up and reveal their true selves; consequently, they don't grow or experience in-depth relationships. They can't. Their souls or deeper feelings are cut off, repressed. As Paul said, the "letter" of the law leads to the death of the soul (2 Cor. 3:6).

Taken to the extreme, legalists become nonpersons, programmed to blindly follow rules. They ask no questions; they dare not or they'll be penalized or rejected. Sadly, most of the rules are man-made. Remember the Jamestown debacle—a tragic case of the blind leading and controlling the over-dependent blind.

On the other hand, relationships are risky. You may feel threatened. You may make mistakes and get hurt. And you may discover some things about yourself that you don't like or want to see. But intimate relationships bring to the surface your weaknesses, giving you the opportunity for dynamic change and growth that hiding behind rules will never give.

One can do all the right things outwardly, have an extensive knowledge of the Scriptures, and have a vital grasp of church doctrine, but fail badly in relating to and loving people.

True Christianity and genuine spirituality cannot be divorced from intimate human relationships. It is only as people work on relationships that they can grow in love towards one another and God. God's Word makes it plain that love for Him reaches perfection only as people love one another (1 John 4:12).

Let Love Be Your Motive

Love is relationships, not rules. Love is unconditional acceptance of others whether they agree with me or not. Love is a commitment to the other person's growth, not his enslavement to my controls. This doesn't imply that we go to the other extreme and disregard rules altogether. Not at all.

Jesus made it clear that He didn't come to destroy the law but to fulfill it (Matt. 5:17). Paul also said that our freedom in Christ wasn't a license to do as we please (Rom. 6:1-2). If I truly love my neighbor I will do the right thing by him. I won't steal from him. I won't lie to him. I won't curse him. I won't gossip about him. And I won't hurt or use him in any way. Therefore, let love be your motive—not guilt or legalism.

Sad to say, too much legalism along with false guilt has been used to try and motivate people to witness for Christ. Both are poor motivators with damaging side effects. Could this be why so many of us "hate" or are afraid to witness? Or why so many of our witnessing programs in the church ultimately seem to break down? As Paul said, man-made guilt (worldly sorrow) produces death and legalism kills the soul (2 Cor. 7:10 and 3:6).

Love is a commitment to the other person's growth—not his enslavement.

To effectively communicate the Christian message is not to follow a set of rules or be motivated by guilt. It is primarily a way of life, and it is at this point that all effective witnessing for Christ needs to commence. This aspect we will take up in the next chapter.

In the meantime, if you feel guilty about your witnessing or lack thereof, acknowledge your feelings, but don't allow them to control or drive you. If you feel you have to go out and witness to someone because that's what a good Christian is supposed to do, may I kindly suggest that you stop. This isn't the Spirit's way. Constraint, yes, but compulsions, no—they are never of God.

God wants you to be freed from this kind of bondage and enslavement. In attacking legalism, Paul wrote, "It is for freedom that Christ has set us free. Stand firm, then, and do not let yourselves be burdened again by a yoke of slavery" (Gal. 5:1).

Remember, only as we are delivered from a "have-to-do-it" spirit are we free to want to communicate our Christian faith.

Questions for Study

1. The author says that guilt is a motivator often used to get people to witness. Do you agree? How has guilt influenced the way you feel about or react to "witnessing"? Do you think the guilt you feel is "false" guilt—that which comes from men, or "true" guilt—that which results from divine judgment? If it is from the Spirit of God can you find Scriptures to support the notion that you are obligated to witness?

2. What is the difference between being motivated by the Holy Spirit and being motivated by guilt? How can you discern between the two?

3. Are inner compulsions from the Holy Spirit or are they from false guilt or other false motivators?

4. What is a compulsion? Can you differentiate between a true conviction and a compulsion?

5. What is the false "external motivator" used to get people to witness for Christ? Why is this a damaging motivator?

6. What is the only true motivator for communicating your Christian faith?

Notes
1. Paul Tournier, *Guilt and Grace*, (New York: Harper and Row Publishers, Inc., 1962), p. 67.
2. Em Griffin, *The Mind Changers*, (Wheaton, IL: Tyndale House Publishers, 1976), p. 62.
3. Ibid, p. 63.
4. Allison C. Fitzsimons, *Guilt, Anger and God*, (New York: Seabury Press, Inc., 1972), p. 12.
5. Griffin, *The Mind Changers*, p. 64.
6. Bruce Larson, *The Relational Revolution*, Waco, TX: Word, Inc., 1976), p. 90.
7. Samuel Bolton, *The True Bounds of Christian Freedom*, (London: The Banners of Truth Trust, 1964 ed.), p. 143.
8. Richard J. Foster, *Celebration of Discipline*, (New York: Harper and Row Publishers, Inc., 1978), p. 8.

Two

BEING VERSUS DOING

Most of my life I was taught that witnessing for Christ was something I did. Simply put, it meant talking about my Christian faith and sharing the plan of salvation whenever I could get or make the opportunity. However, for me this became a real hindrance to effectively communicating Christ, as I was doing it more as an external performance—a learned program—much like a salesman can learn the art of selling a product and master the closing of a sale. As important as sharing the plan of salvation is at the appropriate time, and knowing how to lead a person to Christ, communicating the gospel is a much broader concept than this. In fact, I may be brilliant at telling a person how to receive Christ, but still be a very poor witness and not communicate Christ at all.

More than anything else, communicating Christianity is a way of life. Primarily, it is who I am much more than what I do or say. The key is in first *being* a witness, not merely *doing* a witnessing program.

Perhaps I can explain what I mean in this way.

While I have spent a number of years here in North America, I am an Australian by birth and, having grown up in Australia, my speech has a way of betraying me. "Where are you from?" people often ask me when I meet them. "Are you from England?" most query. A few guess Australia. I've even been told, after saying where I was from, "My, what wonderful English you speak for a foreigner."

Now by virtue of the fact that I am an Australian, I am automatically a witness for my country. I may not choose to be and I may not want to be. I just am. For many Americans I may be the only Australian they've ever met. If they find me distant and not very friendly, they'll no doubt be courteous to me, but they won't feel warm towards me. If I happen to be an *ocker* Australian (loud-mouther, boorish, self-opinionated, arrogant) and insensitive to their feelings, they will undoubtedly take a strong dislike of me. Unfortunately, if I'm the only Australian they've ever met, they will tend to project their negative feelings towards me onto all other Australians whom they have never met and not like them either. And they probably won't ever want to go to Australia.

The opposite is also true. If they find me to be warm and friendly, they will feel drawn to me and like me quite well, and will tend to project their positive feelings towards me onto all other Australians and like them too. I don't have to say one word "of witness" about Australia. They will automatically judge all other Australians on the basis of how they feel towards me and any other Australians they may happen to know.

The same principle operates in my Christian witness. By virtue of the fact that I am a Christian, a member of God's family and a citizen of heaven, without doing anything I am automatically a witness for Jesus Christ and a representative of His kingdom. I don't have to do anything to make myself a witness for Christ. I already am one. I may or may not be a good one, but I am one nevertheless, simply because I am a Christian.

> By virtue of the fact that I am a Christian, I am automatically a witness for Jesus Christ.

Jesus didn't say to His disciples, "After the Holy Spirit is given to you, you will go out and *do* witnessing." He said, "After you receive the Holy Spirit, you will *be* witnesses unto me" (see Acts 1:8).

What you do is important. There's no question about that. But what you are is considerably more important and is by far the most influential. It's like the old adage which says, "What you are speaks so loud I cannot hear what you say."

Just as people like or dislike other Australians according to how they feel towards me, they will also either be drawn to Christ or repelled from Him according to how they feel towards me. If they know I'm a Christian and don't like me for whatever reason, they will tend to project their negative feelings towards me onto all other Christians and will want to withdraw from them and the Christ whom I represent—regardless of whatever I have to say. Worse still, if they don't like me, my words will probably have a boomerang effect and drive them even farther away from Christ.

On the other hand, if people know that I'm a Christian and find me warm, open, and real and they like me, they will then tend to project their positive feelings toward me onto other Christians and feel

WHAT YOU ARE SPEAKS SO LOUD, I CAN'T
HEAR WHAT YOU SAY.

drawn both to them and the Saviour. It's what I am that communicates more about Christianity than anything else.

So the question at this point is not how to do witnessing or how to become a witness. As we've seen, if we're Christians, we're already witnesses. The question is how can we become better witnesses and more effective communicators of Christ's message?

It has been said that Christianity is not merely following a creed but following a Person, experiencing His divine love and forgiveness and communicating that to other people.

To effectively communicate Christ's message of divine love and forgiveness, we therefore need *to be* God's person before *doing* God's work, and thereby establish our credibility to verify our message.

Being God's Person

What I do will very definitely affect people's attitude towards me. There's no question about that. However, I do what I do because I am what I am. As Christ said, I will be known by my fruits (Matt. 7:16); that is, my external actions are an expression of my inner self. Therefore, being the right person or being God's person is more important than doing the right thing or doing God's work. It's akin to what is said about marriage: being the right person is more important than finding the right partner.

By majoring on the part, I missed the whole.

When it comes to the Christian life, doing the "right" thing can actually be the enemy of becoming the right person.

For example, for many years I believed that God's

will for me was primarily what I did, where I did it, and even how much I did of it. So I did what I did with all my might, sincerely believing I was faithfully serving God. But this practice hindered me from finding God's highest will for my life. I couldn't see it at the time, but what I do is only a part of God's will. So for me, by majoring on the part, I missed the whole.

In other words, I was so busy doing God's work that I never saw my need for personal growth. I didn't even know how to grow as a person. And while I was seeing many people making decisions to receive Christ through my ministry, my "success" kept me blind to my need for growth.

To the best of my ability I had surrendered my will and intellect to Christ. From my youth up I had willed to serve Christ with my life and had filled my mind with the knowledge of God's Word and how to do God's work. I thought I had surrendered my heart to Christ and, in a sense, I had done so, but I knew nothing about growing and maturing emotionally, which I have now come to see cannot be separated from growing spiritually. This subject is beyond the scope and purpose of this book; suffice it to say that my doing things for Christ and even studying about Christ kept me blind to my need for growing as a whole person and maturing in Christ. Thus, in my personal and spiritual life, "the good became the enemy of the best."

My performance, however, eventually caught up with me. While appearing to be successful on the outside, I was drying up on the inside and feeling very empty. My personal and family needs were being neglected and my marriage began to suffer. Like so many others, my wife and I were both caught in this trap of doing rather than being, and we have had much growing to do in overcoming our preconditioning.

> Oftentimes it takes a personal setback for us to
> change our values.

In our Western culture we are so programmed to perform that it is difficult to change gears from doing to being. It begins well before we start to school. In our homes, approval is given more on the basis of what we do rather than on who we are. Then throughout all our years of education, on the sports field, in our work, and in our social life, so much emphasis is placed on what we do rather than on who we are. Oftentimes it takes a personal tragedy, a major setback or serious suffering for us to change our values.

Charles W. Colson, ex-hatchet man for President Nixon and founder of Prison Fellowship, said in his address at the one-hundred-twenty-third commencement exercise at Wheaton College that he wasn't proud of the fact that he had been a prisoner, but he did agree with Aleksandr Solzhenitsyn who wrote, "Bless you prison, bless you for having been in my life," after spending ten years in a Soviet prison.

"And," said Colson, "people say that's unthinkable. How could he say that?

"Solzhenitsyn wrote from a prison cell that it was there, lying on that rotting prison straw, that for the first time in his life he understood that the purpose of life is not prosperity as we are made to believe, but the maturing of the human soul."[1]

That is true. In fact, God is much more concerned with our growth and maturity than He is with our doing, or even our happiness. We can do and do and do, but never grow as a person. Only as we grow and mature do we sort out our priorities and begin to do the right things for the right motives.

It isn't God's will to make us good. It is His will to make us mature, for only God is good (Luke 18:19). Any goodness or positive actions will then be an expression or the fruit of our maturity. That is, we are not mature because we do good deeds, but we do good deeds because we are mature. Therefore, God's highest will for our life is not what we do but that we grow to our total God-given human and spiritual potential and become mature in Christ (Col. 1:28). What we do is important, but it is only a part of God's total will for us. It is who we become that is most important to God.

And it is who we are that gives our witness for Christ impact or lack thereof—or what the communicators call *credibility*.

Verifying Our Message

Allan Dollar, pastor of the Sugar Grove Church in Goshen, Indiana, said, "The impact of a message often depends on who says it."

This conviction has been a long accepted belief. Twenty-five hundred years ago Aristotle believed the same thing. He used the Greek term *ethos* referring to the ethical appeal of a speaker to his audience. Thomas M. Scheidel, author of *Speech Communication and Human Interaction*, wrote, "In commenting on *ethos*, or the 'character' of the speaker, Aristotle declared: 'Persuasion is achieved by the speaker's personal character when the speech is so spoken as to make us think him credible. We believe good men more readily than others: This is true generally what-ever the question is, and absolutely true where exact certainty is impossible and opinions are divided . . . . It is not true, as some writers assume in their treatises on rhetoric, that the personal goodness revealed by the speaker contributes nothing to the power of persuasion; on the contrary, his character may almost be called the most effective means of persuasion he possesses.' "[2] Or as Em Griffin expressed it. "If we believe we are listening to a good man, his cause will seem probable."[3]

Perhaps one factor to keep in mind is that a speaker's credibility isn't entirely dependent on who he is but also on who perceives him. No matter how good a person he is, not everybody will listen to or accept his message.

For instance, "The late Adlai Stevenson brought to any interaction with another person an aura of the respect and admiration generally extended to him. His reputation established a form of credibility for him in almost any situation. Moreover, his ability to interact with his fellows in such a way that they felt he had their concern uppermost gave him an even greater, a more dimensional credibility in the minds of his hearers. But even for Stevenson, there were situations (as, for example, a meeting of the John Birch society) in which his credibility would have been low. Credibility is not automatically a function of the individual; the specific situation may be the essential determining factor."[4]

Or, take my youngest son. When he wasn't even four years old yet, he made a statement about something which I tried to correct—in vain. He strongly disagreed with me because his grandmother, according to him, said it was thus and so. I decided not to argue with him because right then on that issue and in his eyes his grandmother had more credibility than I. And as the old saying goes, "A man convinced against his will is of the same opinion still."

However, even though credibility is also in the eyes of the beholder, we can't control that factor. We can only control our own *ethos*. If people like us, they are more likely to give us a hearing. If they don't, we barely stand a chance of gaining a hearing.

We believe good men more readily than others.

I recently had the opportunity of taking a course in public relations. In one field trip we visited two large companies where we were addressed by top men in both firms. Both were highly qualified in their field of expertise. One speaker I really liked and the other I just didn't feel comfortable with. It wouldn't take too much imagination to guess from which man I learned the most. From the speaker I liked I incorporated many ideas into my own philosophy of public relations. From the other speaker I only remembered the points I didn't like.

The application is clear. If we like someone we will more likely listen to him. If we don't like him we will most likely not listen to him. And if we dislike someone strongly, no matter what he says, we will probably be opposed to it.

Avoiding Pitfalls
If we have not already established credibility in the eyes of our audience we could very well affect them in adverse ways. Some of these are described as: the boomerang effect (which we have already mentioned), the regression effect, the sleeper effect and the focusing effect.[5]

The boomerang effect. If a person doesn't like me,

or feels that I am not being completely honest or fair to his point of view, my words may very well backfire. He may not only be opposed to what I am saying, but move farther away from my position, deeper into his own territory of beliefs.

The regression effect. Simply put, this means that if I try to push a person too hard too fast, he may come along with me because of the excitement or emotion of the moment. However, after he has had time to think through things more clearly, he may not be so excited about what I said and then regress to his former position.

I recall on one occasion when I was going to hear a high-powered speaker, I purposely left my wallet and checkbook at home because I knew my heartstrings would be tugged on fairly strongly. I knew that if I made a decision too quickly on what I wanted to give this organization, out of the emotion of the moment, later on I would not be happy with my decision. The same principle holds true when we try to push people into making a decision for Christ before they are ready. Not only do they regress to their former position, but they can become hardened against our cause in the process.

The sleeper effect. This theory or effect can be seen in what happens if I attract people too much to me personally rather than to my cause; that is, if I try to get people to like me too much (which is a problem many of us struggle with, including this writer), I run the risk of their not taking too much notice of my message, or, as time passes, what I had to say will fade from their memory.

A classic example of this was seen in the special one-minute television spots produced by the Christian Television Association in Australia. The spots featured Evie Tornquist Karlsson singing parts of some of her most popular songs. The audience loved the spots. Research showed that in random interviews in places such as shopping centers there was an incredibly high recall; of those watching television at the time Evie was on, 90 percent of the people remembered them. The problem was that it was Evie whom the people loved and remembered. They didn't have any idea twenty-four hours later what her messages were saying. So the spots were discontinued. By the way, that's no offense to Evie. She was singing to a secular audience. I personally love her singing and can recall at least two of her spots several years later.

The focusing effect. In many photographs the foreground is sharply in focus while the background is all hazy because it is out of focus. In presenting the Christian message, if I only show one side of the picture, or only parts of the picture I want the other person to see, or even hide some things, later on the listener is going to wonder about these. As he brings them into focus and looks at them through his own particular lenses, he may in the process get out of focus the picture I have presented. One of the best ways to overcome this problem is to try and present a well-balanced view of the Christian faith, including the negative aspects as well as the positive, and face squarely all of the other person's arguments and doubts—even bringing up some in advance.

To paint too rosy a picture of the Christian life, which has so often been done, is to disillusion people farther down the line. If a person is brought to Christ with the promise or idea that he will not have any more problems, won't get depressed anymore, and will begin on an exciting adventure, what happens when he gets depressed, his wife leaves him, and he loses his job? Many drop out. Where's the exciting adventure now? I'm a Christian too, and oftentimes my life is the pits.

According to Dr. Stephen Olford, 1,400 ministers each year drop out of the Southern Baptist denomination alone.[6] I wonder how many of these drop out because of too rosy a picture painted by those who challenged them to serve God in the ministry in the first place? I personally know this, for when I got into the Christian ministry I had no idea of the struggles ahead! Many a time I feel disillusioned and have felt like quitting too.

> To paint too rosy a picture of the Christian life, is to disillusion people further down the line.

The implications are clear in our presentation of the message of Christ. To verify our message we need credibility. Credibility comes from within. It is who we are much more than what we do or say. If people don't like me, if they feel I'm not entirely straight or honest, if they feel I'm too pushy, if I don't paint a whole picture, or if I try and draw too much attention to myself, in the long run I'll do more to drive them from Christ than draw them to Him.

Identifying with Your Audience

Over the years I have found that the greatest way I can influence others is not through eloquent sermons or clever presentations of the Christian message, but by identifying with my audience and allowing them to see me as I really am—that I am a fellow sinner with human weaknesses just as they are and that I too am in the process and struggle to become the person God wants me to be. I am convinced that only then will people grow. People do not grow through the cognitive process. I may be a great Bible teacher or even a professor of psychology and still be very immature. Knowledge alone doesn't change lives. Growth does. And people only grow as we are open and honest and grow together.

If I come across as the authoritative parent figure or the super teacher who knows all the answers and appears to have it all together, I will have no credibility to make people want to accept my message, to change, or to grow. But if I become vulnerable and show myself as a real flesh-and-blood person, my credibility will rise greatly in their eyes. What I then say will be believable. I have to model what I am saying if I'm going to be credible. As one of my professors, Dr. Glenn Arnold, used to write in red ink on my manuscripts, "Show me, don't tell me!" Simply put, to effectively communicate God's message, I need *to be* God's person and not merely talk about God's message.

As the Apostle Paul said, "When I am with the Jews I seem as one of them so that they will listen to the Gospel and I can win them to Christ. When I am with Gentiles who follow Jewish customs and ceremonies I don't argue, even though I don't agree, because I want to help them. When with the heathen I agree with them as much as I can, except of course that I must always do what is right as a Christian. And so, by agreeing, I can win their confidence and help them too.

"When I am with those whose consciences bother them easily, I don't act as though I know it all and don't say they are foolish; the result is that they are willing to let me help them. Yes, whatever a person is like, I try to find common ground with him so that he will let me tell him about Christ and let Christ save him" (1 Cor. 9:20-22, *TLB*).

Questions for Study

1. What is the difference between *being* a witness for Christ and *doing* witnessing?

2. If what you do is only a part of God's will, what is the other part? Do you agree with this idea? If so, which needs to come first? Why?

3. What are some of the dangers in majoring on "doing all the right" things?

4. Read again the section in this chapter entitled "Avoiding Pitfalls." Can you think of times when your witnessing caused these effects on the people you were witnessing to?

5. How can you raise your own credibility in another's eyes?

Notes

1. Charles W. Colson, "Daring to be Christian," address given at 123rd commencement exercise, Wheaton College, Wheaton, Illinois, May 17, 1982.
2. Thomas M. Scheidel, *Speech Communication and Human Interaction* (Glenview, IL: Scott, Foresman and Company, 1972), pp. 322-323.
3. Emory A. Griffin, *The Mind Changers*, (Wheaton, IL: Tyndale House Publishers, 1976), p. 116.
4. John W. Keltner, *Elements of Interpersonal Communication* (Belmont, CA: Wadsworth Publishing Company, Inc., 1973), pp. 207-208.
5. Thomas M. Scheidel, *Speech Communication and Human Interaction* (Glenview, IL: Scott, Foresman and Company, 1972), pp. 118-119.
6. From an interview with Stephen Olford, president of Encounter Ministries, Wheaton, Illinois, February 19, 1982.

Three

MORE THAN WORDS

Imagine that you've been out of state for several weeks and now you're arriving home. At the airport you see your wife and children there to meet you. The moment they see you, their faces light up. They are obviously delighted that you're home. They push through the crowd of people to greet you. Your wife approaches you with a sparkle in her eyes and a broad smile on her face as she reaches out to hug you.

"It's so good to see you. We've all missed you very much," she says warmly.

But you don't return the smile, your hug is much less than enthusiastic, and in reply to your wife's friendly welcome you say in a cold, flat monotone voice, "I love you. It's good to see you too."

How do you think your wife would feel?

She'd feel terrible and would probably feel like kicking you—and rightfully so.

Even though you've said the three most beautiful words in the English language—I love you—you've told your wife the exact opposite. You have actually communicated, "I don't love you. I am not pleased to see you. And I'm not happy to be home." In other words, your head has said one thing—your heart the opposite.

Words are important, but they are only a small part of the message we are communicating in all of our personal relationships and contacts.

When it comes to presenting the gospel, we can know all the right words, all the proper Scripture verses, have a clear plan of salvation, and say all the right things at the right time, but still present a garbled or conflicting message and leave the listener confused.

Communication is much more than words. It involves the entire personality. To be an effective communicator, therefore, a speaker needs to be aware of the complete message he is presenting. He needs to have his head and his heart both saying the same thing. And he needs to know how to give himself, and not just present a spoken message.

Seeing the Complete Message

In an article on communication, Virginia Satir says, "When judging whether a communication is clear, one must also remember that people communicate in a variety of ways in addition to using words.

"A person simultaneously communicates by his gestures, facial expression, body posture and movement, tone of voice, and even by the way he is dressed."[1] In fact, everything about his entire person and personality communicates a message.

By looking at a person's head and face we can read a lot about what he is saying. If his head is turned away, we feel he is ignoring us or shutting us out. If it is tilted to one side, we wonder what his "angle" is or if he has a hidden agenda. And by looking at his face we can tell whether he is happy or sad, energetic or weary, sick or well, warm or cold, angry or loving. We talk about authentic people being open-faced and secretive people being tight-lipped.

Randall P. Harrison believes that "the head and face are perhaps man's richest sign system. In Western Culture, the head is frequently used in art to represent the whole man; it is seen as the locus of his personality, his intelligence, his soul. The face is central in most communication situations. In fact, we speak of 'face-to-face' communication. Or, the face is used symbolically, as in 'face the music,' or tragically, 'losing face.' "[2]

Even the two sides of the face can say something different. If you take two photographs of a face, one a mirror image of the other, cut them both in half and rematch the photographs with the opposite side of the face from the other photograph, you'll get two somewhat different faces.

It is believed by some that the right side of the face tends to reflect more of one's inner soul and feelings.

However, not only does the face communicate but also the entire body and actions of a person. As Gerard Egan says, "The face and the body are extremely communicative. Even when two people are silent together, the atmosphere can be filled with 'messages.' "[3]

Consider the man who buries himself in the newspaper at the evening meal, or retreats to the television after dinner for the rest of the evening. What is he saying to his wife and children?

Or consider the person who consistently arrives late for his appointments. In some cultures time isn't

COMMUNICATION IS MUCH MORE THAN WHAT YOU SAY.

important. You can arrive one to two hours after the agreed time and still not be late. That's the normal practice. But in Western culture time is a different matter. What is the young man saying to his girl friend when he consistently arrives a half hour or more late for his dates with her?

Identical behavior and identical gestures can of course say different things at different times under different circumstances and in different places. For instance, "A wink of the eye to a beautiful person on a bus means something completely different from a wink of the eye that signifies a put-on or a lie . . . or pounding the fist on the table during a speech in support of a particular politician means something quite different from that same fist pounding in response to news about someone's death."[4]

In Western culture an outstretched arm and hand with palm facing upwards and fingers opening and closing means to come here or is used to hail a taxi. In another culture this can mean, "I want to proposition you." To hail a taxi in that place, one still uses the outstretched arm and hand but the palm of the hand faces downwards. You could appreciate the problems a female missionary from the West had with taxi drivers until she learned why they were being so "friendly."

Or think of the couple who go to bed each night— back to back. They've been doing this for months, perhaps years. One is feeling hurt, the other angry. They say nothing with words but the atmosphere of the whole house broadcasts their animosity towards each other. Unless they learn to put into words what their feelings and actions are saying, they will be heading for serious problems—perhaps divorce.

> Words are important, but they are only a small
> part of the total message being communicated.

In all communication, how a person feels is always communicated, if not in words, then through his tone of voice or any of a hundred nonverbal cues. This is true of a speaker addressing a small group, a large crowd, or in talking to just one person.

As we have already noted, words are important but they are only a small part of the total message being communicated. According to author Albert Mehrabian, they represent only a very small part— only 7 percent of the total message. Of the remaining 93 percent, 38 percent is in the tone of voice and 55 percent is in the nonverbal body language of facial expression, gestures, eye contact, posture, dress, touching, physical closeness or distance, and various actions.[5] (See Figure 1.)

The words spoken are what the speaker is thinking. They represent only 7 percent of the total message. The tone of voice and the nonverbal communication is an expression of what he is feeling. This represents 93 percent of the message and therefore has a much greater impact on the listener that the speaker's words. How the speaker feels simply cannot be hidden.

> If I don't have a genuine concern for you, there's
> no way I can hide my feelings.

As Mehrabian says, "The more you like a person, the more time you are likely to spend looking into his eyes as you talk to him. Standing close to your partner and facing him directly (which makes eye contact easier) also indicates positive feelings."[6] The opposite

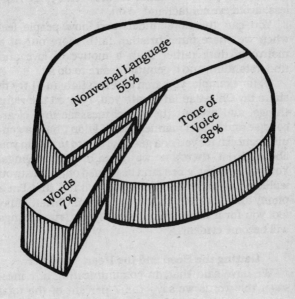

Figure 1
The Complete Message

is also true. If you don't like a person very much, you will tend to put more distance between you, lean away from him rather than toward, tend to be restless, avoid eye contact and so on.

You can therefore understand how people feel when we share our Christian faith more out of a motive of duty rather than a motive of love and understanding and a genuine desire to do so.

If, for example, you aren't a Christian and I try to share my Christian faith with you, I say all the right things, and present the gospel message in a clear, concise and logical manner. But if I don't have a genuine concern for you or a genuine desire to talk to you about Christ, there's no way I can hide my feelings. You will read my "vibes" and be turned off. At best you will leave confused. At worst you will feel that I'm a phony and be driven farther away from Christ. I may fool you for a while, but eventually my true feelings will become evident.

Getting the Head and the Heart Together

We have said that, in communicating any message, the words we say—the 7 percent of the total message—come from the thinking part of the mind. But the nonverbal communication—the 93 percent of the total message—comes from the heart. It is what we feel.

Communication really gets fouled up when what we are saying is not in harmony with what we are feeling. This occurs when we say yes but feel like saying no, or say we want to do something when we don't, or smile sweetly when we are feeling angry, or tell someone we're pleased to see them when we're not.

Or I may say to you, "I think you are beautiful and

intelligent," and thereby lead you to believe that I like you. However, because of your beauty and intelligence, I may feel threatened by you and be jealous of you. If I tell you only what I think, and deny my true feelings, I will act out my feelings in nonverbal ways and tend to withdraw from you. You will then be left wondering what you have said or done or if there is something wrong with you. To communicate effectively with you and to remain close to you, I simply have to tell you not only what I think but also what I feel. This is being an authentic communicator and involves sharing at the feeling level.

This doesn't mean that we need to express what we feel in every situation, but it does mean that we need to be in touch with our feelings and make certain that our words are not out of harmony with our feelings. Only as we are in touch with our inner selves, our feelings, do we make truly effective communicators. This is true not only of singers and musicians but also of speakers, writers, all communicators, including those who expect to be effective witnesses of Christ.

Being open is often difficult, especially for men in our culture where acknowledging feelings tends to be considered feminine—especially warm and tender feelings. This causes many problems in our society. In fact one of the major causes for all unresolved conflicts—especially in marriage and all close relationships—is poor communication. We simply have not learned how to share at the feeling level.

In seminars on personal growth that I conduct I have repeatedly found that the number one complaint from wives on both sides of the Pacific Ocean is this: "My husband doesn't understand my feelings and rarely shares his." Dr. Joyce Brothers agrees. In

"OF COURSE I LOVE YOU, NOW SHUT UP AND
LET ME READ."

The Australian Women's Weekly she reports, "In survey after survey of married women, researchers consistently find that nearly half of them complain that their husbands do not talk to them enough or in any meaningful way."[7]

So, husbands, we desperately need to learn how to communicate effectively at the feeling level, not only in the pulpit, but first in the kitchen and bedroom.

> All communication is effective only to the degree that our words are in harmony with our inner self and feelings.

I asked one man who had come through a long struggle in his marriage what was the secret of his newfound contentment. "I have finally learned to talk meaningfully to my wife about the little things as well as the big things," he said. "We've learned to tell each other what we're thinking and feeling. We now express openly our likes, dislikes, desires, and interests and appreciate each other's point of view. Neither of us has to sacrifice personal identity. We keep the lines of communication open at all times. As a result we've found closeness for the first time."

In her book *Communication in Marriage,* now out of print, Moira Thomas says, "If a person is able to develop a relationship with at least one other human being, in which he can be entirely honest about his feelings, judgments, fears, hopes, beliefs, loves, hates, failures, and successes, he will begin to know himself as a person. This makes him able to show the world the person that he is, without hiding behind a facade that is not really his true self." It also enables him to become an effective communicator.

Whether it is in marriage, in the pulpit, or in one-on-one relationships, or in imparting the gospel as a witness, all communication is effective only to the degree that our words are in harmony with our inner selves and feelings. This makes our witness, our testimony, real. To be effective communicators, we therefore need to be in touch with all of our God-given feelings.

To learn how to get more in touch with your inner selves and feelings, may I suggest that you read several books on this subject; attend a seminar or class such as ACTS conducts on experiential interpersonal communications; join a share group where partici-, pants share feelings and not just ideas; attend a marriage encounter; find a friend with whom you feel safe to share your total self; and start writing your feelings out in a daily journal or in a letter to God such as David did in the Psalms. Do this, and not only will you become a more effective communicator but your own personal life will be greatly enriched and your marriage and interpersonal relationships will be greatly enhanced.

Giving Myself

When I give you only words and tell you what I am thinking I am giving only my ideas and thoughts to you. But when I tell you what I am feeling I am giving *myself* to you. This is the heart of effective communication.

For instance, have you ever wondered why some (certainly not all) singers with magnificent voices leave you cold while other singers with only average voices can move you to tears? What makes the difference? We all know that it is "soul." One gives you his voice and his talent, the other gives himself. He sings from his heart.

The same principle applies to speaking—or writing. The more I am in touch with my inner self and my emotions, the more effective communicator I will be. I need to speak from my heart as well as my head.

This is not sentimentality, a wearing of your heart on your sleeve, or sticky emotionalism—it is authenticity. It is being human, real. The ideal, therefore, is to strive for a balance between the two. Head without heart is cold intellectualism. Heart without head is sticky emotionalism. But head with heart is realism.

A person who is authentic is a person who is in touch with all of his God-given emotions. The more he is able to experience and admit his feelings of fear, anger, and pain, the more he is able to experience his feelings of love, wonder, and joy and communicate these. When the authentic person communicates, his head and his heart are saying the same thing. His message is genuine. He is believable.

On the other hand, the non-authentic person who has many of his feelings repressed, is a closed person. He reflects "an emotional deadness marked by a loss of spontaneity and responsiveness."[8] He builds barriers around himself and often acts outwardly the opposite of what he is feeling inwardly. For example, the saccharine sweet person is usually a very angry person, but as he is unwilling or unable to accept himself as being angry, he acts out the opposite role. But he's never quite believable.

Emotionalism too, like saccharine sweetness, is a defense against true emotion. When a person is hiding feelings he doesn't like he may overreact by becoming too emotional. This way his surface feelings serve as a cover of his deeper feelings which he is afraid to accept and face. He is only believable by his own kind—that is, by those who use emotionalism as a defense against their true feelings.

Another person may hide his inner feelings by outwardly acting very cool or intellectual. But when he talks, he talks only from his head and not his heart. He leaves you unmoved.

> Intellectual concepts in and of themselves do not motivate people to change or grow.

At one particular public meeting I attended with my family, the speaker was very articulate and outwardly pleasant, but I particularly remember this occasion not because of what the speaker said, but because of what my then twelve-year-old son said. "What a phoney," he remarked. One of my non-Christian friends was a little more gracious in his response, but basically said the same thing. "I felt he was a professional," he remarked, as he dismissed the speaker's attempts to win him to the Christian faith. To me this speaker did not seem to be in touch with his inner self and therefore came across as not being quite real.

There was nothing wrong with what the speaker said. His doctrine, theology, and teaching were fine. But divorced from his inner self they remained intellectual concepts, and intellectual concepts in and of themselves do not motivate people to change or grow. Motivation comes from the heart.

There's an old ditty that goes like this:

> I often say my prayers, but do I really pray,
> And does the meaning of my heart go with
> the words I say?

And that about sums up the heart of all effective

communication. Whether I am talking to God, my spouse, or my neighbor, I need to be certain that the meaning of my heart is in harmony with the words I am saying. This makes my words believable. And to be believable, I just need to be real.

Questions for Study

1. If, as the author says, 55 percent of communication depends on nonverbal language, how valuable are memorized witnessing formats?

2. What percentage of any communication is found in the actual words?

3. From what part of a speaker's personality come his tone of voice and nonverbal language?

4. What happens to a listener when the speaker's words are not in harmony with his nonverbal language?

5. If a speaker (or writer) is not in touch with his own inner self/feelings, will his effectiveness as a communicator be dulled? Why?

6. What makes a speaker's words believable?

7. Jesus said that we would recognize a false prophet (or witness) by his fruits (Matt. 7:15-20). Since the Christian witness is to reflect the Holy Spirit within him, what are the fruits of the Spirit as Paul names them in Galatians 5:22-25?

Notes

1. Thomas M. Steinfatt, *Readings in Human Communications,* (Indianapolis: Bobbs-Merrill Educational Publishing, 1977), p. 347.
2. Ibid., p. 167.
3. Gerard Egan, *Interpersonal Living,* (Monterey, CA: Brooks/Cole Publishing Company, 1976), p. 98.
4. Joseph A. DeVito, *The Interpersonal Communication Book,* 2nd ed. (New York: Harper and Row Publishers, Inc., 1980), p. 240.
5. Albert Mehrabian, *Silent Messages,* (Belmont, CA: Wadsworth Publishing Company, Inc., 1971), pp. 42-44.
6. Steinfatt, *Readings,* p. 142.
7. Joyce Brothers, "How to Make Your Husband Really Talk to You," *The Australian Women's Weekly.* vol. 46, no. 27. December 1978, p. 20.
8. Dick Williams, "More Than Just Talking," *Restore,* October 1981, p. 12.

Four

DARE TO BE HONEST

Terry and Lynne George have been involved in ACTS International for at least ten years—almost since its inception. Terry is now the chairman of the Australian board of directors and Lynne is our staff artist. She is also in charge of our printing and production and is responsible for preparing a considerable amount of outreach literature that is being used by hundreds of churches throughout Australia, New Zealand and now in the United States as well.

Lynne wasn't a Christian when she joined our staff. I was overseas at the time. She didn't know me, nor I her. From what one might expect, she could have been completely turned off to Christianity because of something I did soon after we met. This would have pleased Terry as his attitude towards church people at the time wasn't what one would call favorable. "Whatever you do," he said to Lynne, "just don't get too involved with a bunch of religious nuts!"

However, what happened is this: Soon after I met Lynne, she overheard me talking to two salesmen. I didn't know she was nearby. I felt these men were trying to do a con job on me. I became angry, and expressed my feelings explicitly.

What I said wasn't that important, but how Lynne reacted was. She went home and said to Terry, "I can't believe my new boss. He's supposed to be a minister. He said such-and-such. He's real." Only a few months ago—ten years later—Lynne told me that this was the very thing that motivated her and Terry to become Christians.

Surprised? Don't we have the idea that as Christians we're supposed to be all nice and flowery if we're going to be good witnesses? It isn't true. Perhaps more than anything else people want us to be real— to be human. If we come over as being "holier than thou" or with our head in the "biblical clouds," we simply turn people off.

To be effective communicators of Christ's message we need to be ordinary human beings who are realistic about ourselves and about life, and above all, honest and authentic persons.

Christianity is for sinners, not "saints." It is for those who recognize and admit their weaknesses and know that they need a power outside of themselves if they're going to make it. It is for those who are in the process of growth and maturity. It isn't for those who have it all together, because nobody does. Those who act as if they do, make poor communicators. This doesn't mean we blatantly sin or that we are not to strive to live upright lives. Not at all (Rom. 6:1-2). It means we are to strive for maturity which will produce mature actions and not merely act out a superficial and unreal type of religious experience.

"You know what affected me most?" said a young woman whom Rebecca Pippert was seeking to win to

Christ. "All my life I used to think, 'How arrogant for someone to call himself a Christian, to think he's that good.' But then I got to know you—and Becky, you are far from perfect, yet you call yourself a Christian. So my first shock was to discover you blow it like I do. But the biggest shock was that you admitted it, where I couldn't. Suddenly I saw that being a Christian didn't mean never failing, but admitting when you've failed. I wanted to keep Christ in a box and let you be religious during Bible studies. But the more you let me inside your life, the more impossible it became to keep the lid on Christianity. Even your admission of weakness drove me to Him!"[1]

> To be effective witnesses . . . we need to be honest and realistic . . . anything less is being a false witness.

All too often, however, our Christian witness and message is blatantly unrealistic and far too simplistic. We pretend to be what we're not. We paint such a rosy picture of the Christian life that it becomes unreal. We then pressure others to conform to our unrealistic expectations and become afraid to be authentic ourselves.

We sing songs like, "Every day with Jesus is sweeter than the day before," or "I'm so happy here's the reason why, Jesus took my burdens all away." They sound great but they simply are not realistic. Our non-Christian friends know it too. Becoming a Christian doesn't necessarily make a person happy or take away his burdens. It doesn't destroy his humanity. Being human we sometimes have terrible days. And some of our burdens will not be taken away until we get to eternity.

"PASTOR, THANKS FOR TELLING US YOU WERE COMING."

Even in many of our more dignified hymns the same sentiment is expressed. Wade Robinson wrote,

Heaven above is softer blue,
earth around is sweeter green;
Something lives in every hue
Christless eyes have never seen!

This is indeed a beautiful hymn, but it is only partially true. For Robinson it was undoubtedly true, but to imply that the non-Christian doesn't see the beauty of nature and is not deeply moved when he beholds the greatness of the heavens or watches a beautiful sunset just isn't true or fair. And to imply that becoming a Christian automatically gives a person a deep appreciation of nature isn't true either. Falling in love can have the same effect.

Appreciation of God's creation is more dependent on whether or not a person is in touch with his emotions of wonder and awe. If these emotions are repressed, he won't be moved deeply by nature. Falling in love or becoming a Christian won't make too much difference.

The point I'm making is this. To be effective witnesses for Christ, and effective communicators of His message, we need to be honest and realistic in our statements as well as with ourselves. Anything less is being a false witness.

What Makes People Unreal?

There are many reasons Christians have trouble being real. They are all basically motivated by fear— fear of public pressure, fear of being known, fear of rejection, fear of God, fear of parents, and so on.

Fear of public pressure. In our society there can

be a tremendous amount of pressure to conform. Conformity is often the password for acceptance. John Simpson, a friend of mine, has a sharp mind and thinks for himself. But this causes him difficulties on occasion. He said to me recently that his own needs for acceptance were so strong that he simply did not have the courage to step outside the accepted norms in his particular church and say what he thought, even though he felt strongly that the group was wrong in some instances.

It can be very difficult to be real and stand up for truth. Many a man or woman who follows the beat of his or her own drum is going to be lonely and isolated at times.

Lyman Coleman feels the same say. "We are said to be a society dedicated, among other things, to the pursuit of truth," he writes. "Yet, disclosure is often penalized. Impossible concepts of how men ought to be—which sadly enough are often handed down from the pulpit—make man so ashamed of his true being that he feels obliged to seem different . . . yet, when a man is out of touch with reality, he will sicken and die; and no one can help him without access to the facts."[2]

Or think of the pressure put on people who step way outside the accepted norms of belief or practice. Galileo (1564-1642) was a man who thought for himself and came to his own conclusions. Imagine the reaction he received when everybody else in the entire world believed that the sun revolved around the earth and he claimed that it was the other way around. Sad to say, his greatest opposition came from the church who "maintained that human beings had a unique and favored relationship to God; therefore, they and the earth had to be the center of things. Galileo was forced to recant in public, and until his death was forbidden to take part in further public discussion on religious or political matters."[3]

At about the same time, in the 1600s, Anne Hutchinson of Boston challenged the Puritan thinking and theology of her day. She opposed religious dogma and the practice of "denying women a voice in the church . . . . She openly provoked others, including women, to do the same. For this she suffered a long, miserable trial, was convicted of heresy, excommunicated, and sent into the wilderness for punishment. Eventually she and her family were massacred."[4]

One lone woman, Mary Dyer, was the only person to speak in defense of Anne Hutchinson. But twenty-two years later she met a similar fate. She was hanged as a Quaker by the Boston fathers.[5]

While these are extreme cases, they do point out the fact that it can be very threatening and difficult to be true to yourself. Unfortunately, so much of what we believe and do is done in the light of what others will think of us. Thus we are not being true to ourselves and are being controlled not by the Holy Spirit but by others and our own need for their approval.

Fear of being known. A fear of knowing ourselves and being known by others is another reason we find it difficult to be authentic. I am afraid that if I know me as I really am, I might not like me. And if you know me as I really am, I'm afraid that you mightn't like me either.

I heard one highly respected Bible teacher (who founded a Bible College in Australia and lectured in a seminary overseas) actually teach that people should confess their sins only to God and not to anybody else. And yet this is in direct contradiction to what the Bible teaches. "Get into the habit of admitting your sins to one another," James states (Jas. 5:15, *Phillips*); so that you can pray for one another).

Em Griffin feels that "this is the most ignored bit of advice I know of in Scripture, probably because we're afraid that people won't like us or trust us when they see how crummy we really are. But the reverse is true. They've got the same sin problem. As we openly reveal our innermost struggles, the plastic masks we wear begin to slip. Human warmth escapes and people begin to respond in trust."[6]

"Only sinners can relate."

As long as I deny my own reality and my sinfulness, I cannot truly relate to other people nor can I effectively communicate Christ. As Richard C. Halverson, chaplain of the U.S. Senate says, "Only sinners can relate.

"Sinners enjoy authentic fellowship. Saints don't!

"People who pose as saints aren't free to remove their masks.

"Under pressure to project conventional piety, they are unable to open up and share themselves.

"Upholding the traditional religious image, they remain invulnerable in human relationships because they dare not expose their real selves.

"They major in propositions rather than persons . . . share their victories but never their failures . . . congratulate one another in their little mutual admiration society.

"Meeting head to head instead of heart to heart, protecting themselves against discovery, they ricochet against each other like marbles.

"The authentic saint is oblivious to his sainthood,

deeply aware of his unworthiness, sensitive to his failure, confesses he is a sinner, which makes possible true fellowship.

"Sinners acknowledge their inadequacy, lean heavily on God's grace, and identify quickly with need in others.

"Recognizing all men are sinners, unwilling to hide from the truth, they share their weaknesses, confess their sin to one another, and do not fear vulnerability.

"They come together like grapes, crushed and fragrant, dependent upon each other, and God."[7]

I've often wondered about David being a man after God's own heart. I'm sure it wasn't because of his behavior patterns. Not only was he guilty of committing adultery with Bathsheba, but in order to cover his sin, he had her husband, Uriah, killed when he discovered Bathsheba was pregnant (2 Sam. 11:1-17). How could *he* be a man after God's own heart? Because he was honest with his inner self and was willing to confess his sins and express his feelings (see Ps. 51).

It was David who wrote that God desires truth in the innermost being. "You deserve honesty from the heart; yes, utter sincerity and truthfulness. Oh, give me this wisdom" (Ps. 51:6, *TLB*).

Fear of rejection. Many of us would never dream of cheating on our income tax or even telling a white lie, but we can be incredibly ingenious when it comes to hiding our true feelings and inner selves. We can be masters at pretending to be what we're not.

The Wilson family would be typical of many of us. The entire family knew how much Fred hated being late for church, and here they were, late again. The third Sunday in a row.

Fred was furious but wouldn't admit it. Mary, his wife, became very tense and the children slunk in the back seat. The atmosphere in the car all the way to church was filled with negative vibes. Nobody said a word.

But the moment the Wilsons pulled up in the church parking lot and stepped out of their car, a sudden transformation took place. Fred pushed his "dignified deacon" button, and Mary pushed her "happy Christian" button. Like many of the rest of us, the Wilsons were afraid that if they became known as they really were, they wouldn't be liked. So they repressed their real selves and their negative feelings, and pretended to be something outwardly that they weren't feeling inwardly.

I'm not suggesting that we go around wearing our hearts on our sleeves, but I am suggesting that problems, conflicts, and feelings need to be faced and resolved and not iced over. The danger in the Wilsons' type of life-style is that when hiding from one's real self becomes an unconscious and automatic way of life, emotional and spiritual growth ceases. As Peter admonished, "Don't just pretend to be good! Be done with dishonesty . . . . Long to grow up" (1 Pet. 2:1-2, *TLB*).

In fact, only as a person stops pretending to be something that he isn't, and allows himself to become fully known as he is, can he grow as a well integrated, whole personality.

"People's selves stop growing when they repress them."

In his book *The Transparent Self,* Sidney Jourard explains: "When I say that self-disclosure is a means by which one achieves personality health, I mean that it is . . . not until I am my real self (and act my real self) that my real self is in a position to grow. One's self grows from the consequence of being. People's selves stop growing when they repress them."[8]

Fear of God. This problem of hiding and repressing one's self is a part of our fallen, sinful nature. It goes right back to Adam. When he sinned he felt guilty and exposed, so he hid himself. He was afraid of rejection by God. When God called to him, "Where are you?" he replied, "I was afraid because I was naked; so I hid." (Gen. 3:9-10). He then proceeded to defend himself by projecting the blame onto somebody else. In this case he said that it wasn't only the woman's fault, but God's fault. "The woman *you* gave me made me do it," he inferred.

That is what sin and negative feelings tend to do to all of us. We become afraid of being exposed for what we truly are inside—either for what we have done or for what we feel. We feel naked also, so we run for cover and hide our true selves and become defensive. We are afraid that if others see us as we really are, they won't like or accept us, so over the years we slowly build up masks and defenses and hide behind them. We thus project, unconsciously, an outer image to mislead people into thinking that we are something that we aren't.

The great tragedy is that first we hide from God. Then we hide from others. And ultimately we hide from ourselves until we no longer know who or what we really are. It is possible to bury and deny our feelings for so long that we are no longer aware that they exist, and to live with our masks for so long that we come to believe that our outer public image is the real self. Little by little we cut our feelings off and become

closed as persons, emotionally dishonest and non-
authentic. Eventually we begin to dry up, feel empty
or lonely, become cold and mechanical as persons, or
become physically ill. And as communicators of
Christ's love we become totally ineffective. We may
communicate a message about Christ, but we don't
communicate Christ, and there is a world of difference between the two.

Fear of parents. A major cause for hiding our feelings is that many of us as children were never allowed
to express our feelings, especially the negative ones.
We were taught never to lie to our parents or other
people, but at the same time were not allowed to say
how we felt. Negative feelings were not acceptable.
Thus we were taught to deny these feelings and lie to
ourselves, which is just as sinful as lying to another
person—perhaps even more sinful and destructive.
And in the process of denying negative feelings, positive feelings got repressed as well.

Dr. Cecil Osborne, author and counselor, finds
that "many people bury feelings which they find
unacceptable. For instance, one learned as a child
that hate, greed, jealousy, fear and lust, were 'bad.'
'You shouldn't feel that way,' is the message which
the child received, verbally or otherwise. By a clever
bit of unconscious dishonesty one may have said to
himself, for instance, 'A Christian never hates. I am a
Christian, therefore I never feel hatred.' And the
aggression which is part of the normal equipment of
an average human being is then buried in the unconscious, only to come out in some unacceptable form,
often as a physical symptom."[9]

Consequences of Being Repressed

There are many negative consequences of being

dishonest with our feelings, not the least of which is the fact that it is one of the worst enemies of effective communication. There is no way we can effectively communicate God's truth to anyone if we are not authentic persons. There are other dangers as well.

Destroys spiritual and personal growth. Cecil Osborne believes that "it is highly important that one become aware of his emotions in order to become a well integrated individual. There can be little hope of spiritual growth unless we are willing to deal with our God-given capacity to feel deeply. One can become emotionally and spiritually mature only as he becomes willing to let the deep emotions operate as God intended. This does not refer to 'becoming emotional,' but having a conscious awareness of all our feelings."[10]

To truly relate to God, He requires "truth in the inner parts" (Ps. 51:6). Peter, we have said, pointed out that a part of growing up into the fulness of Christ was to "be done with dishonesty" (1 Pet. 2:1, *TLB*). And Paul said that as Christians we need to speak truly, deal truly, and live truly "and so become more and more in every way like Christ" (Eph. 4:15, *TLB*).

> "How can I love a person whom I do not know? How can the other person love me if he doesn't know me?"

Destroys personal relationships. Sidney Jourard also points out that "alienation from one's real self not only arrests one's growth as a person, it also tends to make a farce out of one's relationships with people . . . . A self-alienated person—one who does not disclose himself truthfully and fully—can never love another person nor can he be loved by another person. Effective loving calls for knowledge of the object . . . . How can I love a person whom I do not know? How can the other person love me if he does not know me? . . . A truly personal relationship between two people involves disclosure of self one to the other in full and spontaneous honesty."[11]

I am sure that this is what John means when he tells us to "walk in the light" (1 John 1:7), that is, walk in honesty and openness with each other and God. Only then can we have true fellowship one with the other and with God.

It is destructive to relationships when we highly censor our communications with each other and do not allow our true feelings to show. In so doing we allow hidden walls and barriers to build up between ourselves and others. Eventually our warm feelings of love and friendship are blocked out.

In his chapter, "Being a Nice Guy Gets You Nowhere," Alan McGinnis says that "there is a man we treat often in psychiatric clinics. You have known him, for he is everywhere. He may even be a member of your family. I'm referring to the 'nice guy!' He smiles a great deal, is cheerful with everyone, never quarrels or gets angry, appears to be universally liked, and might be supposed to have several deep friendships. But as a matter of fact, such persons not only develop a host of psychological problems, but they also tend to mess up their important relationships."[12]

The problem with this fellow is that he isn't real, and while he may be superficially liked by everyone, he isn't deeply loved by anyone. Being popular can be a far cry from being intimate. This is one reason why some very popular people are also very lonely.

The person who is cheerful all the time isn't real. Life simply isn't like that. If he can't show his negative feelings he can't show his positive feelings either. He may show sentiment, perhaps, but not love. He just doesn't ring true. McGinnis says that "the nice guy is pleasant to be around at first, but in the long run most of us prefer the company of people with passion. They may aggravate us at times, but at least they do not bore. Without knowing it, he poisons his relationships with his passive hostility."[13]

> "People who cannot reveal themselves appropriately run the risk of impoverished lives and a wide variety of neurotic disorders."

Destroys mental and physical health. Doctors all agree that unresolved inner and personal conflict—much of which is caused by being closed as persons and having supercharged repressed negative emotions—is a major cause or contributing factor in many of our mental and physical sicknesses.

Gerard Egan points out that extensive discussions, "based on both theory and research, indicate that people who cannot reveal themselves appropriately run the risk of impoverished lives and a wide variety of neurotic disorders."[14]

Egan also quotes Sidney Jourard as saying that every maladjusted person is a person "who has not made himself known to another human being and in consequence does not know himself. Nor can he be himself. More than that, he struggles actively to avoid becoming known by another human being. He works at it ceaselessly, twenty-four hours daily, and it is work!"[15]

And this work takes considerable energy. A

repressed person often tires easily and easily wears himself out or alternatively burns himself out. Besides upsetting the chemical balance of his body, which seriously affects his health, his resistance to sickness is lowered because he wears himself out. He's so uptight because he's keeping his feelings under such tight control.

"Psychologists disagree about almost everything," says Alan McGinnis, "but on one point they display surprising unanimity: There is no such thing as a person who never gets angry—there are only those who suppress anger. And sending anger underground [and any other negative emotion] can produce a thousand psychosomatic problems, such as ulcers, migraines, and hypertension, and also some serious relational difficulties."[16]

> Being repressed is . . . also destructive of interpersonal and public communications.

Destroys effective communications. Being repressed is not only damaging to personal and spiritual growth, personal relationships, emotional and physical health, but it is also destructive of interpersonal and public communications.

For example, I might be a brilliant public speaker, but if I'm not in touch with my feelings, my words simply do not jell if I'm trying to talk about love and life and Christianity. Talking about mechanics is something different. I can be mechanical. But to talk about life, I need to be in touch with life. And if I'm not, and you are, you will quickly sense whether I'm for real or not. Just like Christ knew that Nathanael was a man without guile the moment He saw him. "Here is a true Israelite, in whom there is nothing false," He said as Nathanael approached Him (John 1:47).

If you sense that I'm not authentic and that my words don't ring true, you will tune me out immediately.

However, it is difficult given the background of our Western culture to be open with our feelings and transparent with our inner selves. Almost all of our training and experience is centered at the cognitive or thinking level of the mind. Matters of the heart and feelings have been sadly neglected and even belittled as being unimportant. Fortunately, this emphasis is changing, but many of us still find it difficult, if not impossible, to communicate our feelings and inner selves.

In fact, author John Powell's view is that "most of us feel that others will not tolerate such emotional honesty in communication. We would rather defend our dishonesty on the grounds that it might hurt others, and, having rationalized our phoniness into nobility, we settle for superficial relationships."[17]

However, if we're not open and honest with ourselves and other people, we can't be open and honest with God either. "Consequently, we ourselves do not grow, nor do we help anyone else to grow. Meanwhile we have to live with repressed emotions—a dangerous and self-destructive path to follow. Any relationship which is to have the nature of true personal encounter must be based on this honest, open, gut-level communication. The alternative is to remain in my prison, to endure inch-by-inch death as a person."[18]

How to Be Authentic
The problem is, how does one learn to be honest

with his inner self and become a more authentic person?

It isn't easy. For many of us, even knowing what we're feeling is like learning a new language. But it can be learned. There are no "four simple steps," as personal honesty is more a state of being than of doing. However, there are some principles to follow and actions to take.

Admit your sinfulness. Personal honesty begins when one is honest enough to admit that he has a few problems or areas for personal growth he needs to be working on.

As John reminds us, "If we claim to be without sin, we deceive ourselves and the truth is not in us" (1 John 1:8). And if we say we have no problems we also deceive ourselves.

Confess your weaknesses. One then needs to seek out a trusted friend with whom he can share his whole self without any fear of judgment—a friend who will accept him just as he is, the way God accepts him.

One can begin practicing openness with this friend by confessing the things he does know are wrong in his life and then by asking God to give him the courage to face and confess his hidden sins, faults, false motives, and buried feelings.

> Most people don't want to face inner feelings until they are hurting sufficiently and want to change.

Look at your symptoms. While the eyes are supposed to be the window to the soul, symptoms are even more so. They are often the clues to inner needs. An impaired relationship, a dull marriage, stress, anxiety, depression, or a physical symptom is often caused by an unresolved inner problem. Ulcers, for example, can be caused by repressed fears or other negative emotions. Arthritis can be caused by unresolved resentment. Many years ago the psalmist wrote, "My health is broken beneath my sins . . . because of my sins I am bent and racked with pain . . . my whole body is diseased (Ps. 38:3,6,7 *TLB*). Sin, of course, is much more than overt action. Sin is anything less than wholeness—it is unresolved inner conflicts, damaged emotions, impaired relationships, repressed emotions, and so on.

Is it any wonder Paul in Ephesians 4:26 wrote, "Do not let the sun go down while you are still angry" or "don't sin by nursing your grudge" (*TLB*), and Peter said, "So get rid of your feelings of hatred. Don't just pretend to be good!" (1 Pet. 2:1, *TLB*). Grudges, hatred, resentment, and all forms of anger, guilt and other repressed negative emotions poison personal relationships and physical health.

Other clues to inner repressed feelings are: lacking in love; being bored with life in general; feeling inner dryness; showing coldness of heart; having sexual problems; feeling lonely; feeling inadequate; being supersensitive; lacking self-worth; feeling guilt; harboring phobias; withdrawing when feeling hurt; overreacting; becoming easily angered; being anxious; having a drinking, smoking, or overeating problem; working too much without relaxation; showing an austere bearing; being overtalkative; overcompensating in anything, and a score of others.

Ask God to help you. If you have any symptoms at all, you can ask God to help you trace your symptoms to the inner causes. It helps to ask God for courage and insight to do so. Also, if you are too afraid or unable to face your inner feelings, you can tell God that you are willing to be made willing.

God's answer may come in unexpected ways. Most people have spent years building walls around their inner selves and those walls don't come down quickly or easily. Help may come through a friend, a book, a share group, a counselor, a personal setback, a difficult relationship, loss of a love object, sickness, etc., etc.

Unfortunately, most of us don't want to face inner feelings until we are hurting sufficiently and want to change. Growth and change just happen to be painful. As the saying goes, "No pain—no gain."

Accept yourself as human. We also need to accept ourselves as normal human beings who have a whole spectrum of emotions ranging from love, joy, peace, through to fear, hurt, anger, and so on. These are all God-given emotions without which life would be incredibly dull. To be thankful for our emotions can help us accept them. It is also interesting to note that Jesus never told people how to feel—only how to act or how to handle our feelings.

Learn to express your feelings. The more you verbalize the feelings you are aware of, the more you will increase your sensitivity to all your feelings. When you are feeling hurt, afraid, or angry, say, "I feel hurt," or "I feel angry," never, "You hurt me," or "You make me angry," as this is blaming the other person for your own feelings. Feelings need to be accepted and owned to be resolved, as our reactions are always our own responsibility.

Feelings can also be written out as David so often did in the Psalms. See Psalm 109 for example.

When expressing feelings, however, there is a higher law than the law of honesty, and that is the law of love. Nevertheless, where love reigns, people will be honest with one another but they will always strive to speak "the truth in love" (Eph. 4:15).

The Spirit of Truth

"Speaking truly, dealing truly, living truly" is what makes a person authentic. And being authentic along with being filled with the Holy Spirit is what makes the Christian communicator truly effective. However, we can only be filled with the Holy Spirit to the degree that we are truthful with our inner selves. The Holy Spirit is the Spirit of truth (John 16:13).

Only as we are truthful can we be filled with the Spirit of truth. The areas of our lives which we keep closed to ourselves and others, we also keep closed to God and the Holy Spirit.

To be an effective Christian communicator, therefore, we need to be open and honest with ourselves, with others and with God.

There is no other way.

Questions for Study

1. What does it mean to be an authentic person? Why is it important to be so?

2. The author lists five reasons why Christians might have trouble being real. Which of these could apply to you? Read 1 John 4:16-18. How do we rid ourselves of fear and consequently of falseness?

3. If a person is closed to himself with many of his God-given emotions repressed, can he truly be open to God, the Holy Spirit and others? What reasons do you have for your conclusion?

4. How can you begin today to learn to be authentic? Review again the "principles to follow" in the section "How to Be Authentic."

Notes

1. Rebecca Manley Pippert, *Out of the Saltshaker and into the World*, (Downers Grove, IL: Inter-Varsity Press, 1979), pp. 29-30.
2. Walden Howard, comp., *Groups That Work*, (Grand Rapids: Zondervan Publishing House, 1967), p. 23.
3. Muriel James and Dorothy Jongeward, *Born to Win*, (Reading, MA: Addison-Wesley Publishing Company, 1971), p. 74.
4. Ibid.
5. Ibid.
6. Emory A. Griffin, *The Mind Changers*, (Wheaton: Tyndale House Publishers, Inc., 1976), p. 131.
7. Richard C. Halverson, "Only Sinners Can Relate," *Encounter*, May 1978, p. 2.
8. Sidney M. Jourard, *The Transparent Self*, rev. ed., (New York: D. Van Nostrand Company, Inc., 1971), p. 32.
9. Cecil G. Osborne, *Leader's Handbook*, (Burlingame: Yokefellows, Inc.), p. 32.
10. Ibid.
11. Jourard, *Transparent Self*, pp. 25-28.
12. Alan Loy McGinnis, *The Friendship Factor*, (Minneapolis: Augsburg Publishing House, 1979), p. 128.
13. Ibid., p. 129.
14. Gerard Egan, *Interpersonal Living*, (Monterey, CA: Brooks/Cole Publishing Company, 1976), p. 40.
15. Ibid., p. 41, quoted from Jourard, *The Transparent Self*, 1971, pp. 32-33.
16. McGinnis, *Friendship Factor*, p. 128.
17. John Powell, *Why Am I Afraid To Tell You Who I Am?*, (Niles, IL: Argus Communications, 1969), p. 61.
18. Ibid.

Five

BE CHRIST

A few years ago I took a spiritual and psychological test which indicated that I had a repressed fear. This troubled me, as repressed fear can express itself in many ways, most of which are self-defeating. For instance, if I have a fear of failure I can unconsciously set myself up to fail. If I have a fear of rejection I can repeatedly set myself up to get or feel rejected. If I have a fear of love through being hurt in the past I may not let myself get too close to anyone for fear of being hurt again. Or my repressed fear may express itself in an annoying phobia.

When I discovered I had a repressed fear, I immediately prayed, "Lord, I want to face that fear. Please help me to see what it is."

Eventually my fear surfaced to consciousness. But it took two years and some painful experiences to get through my defenses, as I had buried that fear deep in my subconscious memory.

At the time, I was involved in a counselor training program and was with a group of twelve students. We took turns in counseling each other. At one point one of the students was counseling me. For some reason unknown to both of us she triggered some very deep grief in me and I began weeping uncontrollably.

"Why am I crying?" I asked Sue.

"I don't know," she said, "but just keep crying."

I must have been sobbing for an hour or more when I looked up into Sue's face. What I saw took me totally by surprise. Many years before, at the age of five, I had a sister who was only eighteen months old when she took ill suddenly, was rushed to the hospital, and died. In Sue's face I saw my little sister Margaret.

By the time my sister died I had already learned that "big men" don't cry and had learned to laugh off my troubles. On the day of her funeral when somebody asked me how I was, I simply laughed it off and said I was doing fine. But my sister and I were very close and loved each other dearly, so what happened to all that grief?

For over thirty years it remained hidden and repressed. As John Powell says, whenever we bury negative feelings, we never bury them dead but very much alive. Along with that buried grief was a deep fear of love. "If you love someone," my childish mind had unconsciously reasoned, "you might lose them. So don't ever let yourself get too close to anyone again."

Once I expressed all that buried grief, I was able to face and resolve my hidden fear. As Christ said, "You will know the truth, and the truth will set you free" (John 8:32). However, in the process of expressing my grief, something else unusual happened. Sue, my counselor, gave me no advice. She didn't tell me to cheer up or that I shouldn't feel the way I did. Mercifully, she just gave me permission and encouragement to weep out my pain. More than that, at one point she sat on the floor and wept with me.

Again I looked into her face. Once again I was completely taken by surprise. This time I saw in her face the face of Jesus. He came into focus for a moment then quietly faded away.

Here was a person who identified with me in my suffering. She wept with me, and in that loving act I saw Christ.

"Lord, please help me *be Christ* to somebody today."

That experience had a profound impact on my attitude about witnessing for Christ. I have many times since asked myself the question: "I wonder if people ever 'see' Christ in me?" If they don't, my words won't be of too great a value.

And now, while I don't always remember to pray the following prayer every day, I like to: "Lord, I don't ask so much that you will give me the opportunity to talk to somebody about you today, but rather, please help me *be Christ* to somebody today."

To *be Christ* to somebody can be vastly different than just talking about Him. Em Griffin captures this same idea when he suggests that we should not only sing, "What a Friend we have in Jesus," but also, "What a Jesus we have in friends."

How can we be Christ to others?

Be a Friend

Perhaps one of the best ways we can be Christ

**"DON'T TRY TO UNDERSTAND ME,
JUST LOVE ME."**

to someone is by being a true friend. We can be this in many ways.

Be an encourager. Many people around us are hurting, lonely, suffering and in need of a friend who cares. They need someone who can reach out and touch them, not merely physically but emotionally. Someone who can encourage them to share their feelings, to listen to them and accept them just as they are.

To encourage means to put courage into another. And that's something we all need lots of.

Be nonjudgmental. Do people around us trust us with their innermost struggles and problem? Or do they fear we will be critical of them? A friend of mine was involved in a problem that he was feeling guilty about but was too afraid to share with anyone for fear of being rejected.

"Why do you need this problem?" was all I said to him and dropped the matter.

When next I saw him I asked him how he was getting along. He said he kept thinking about my question and realized that he didn't need that problem and was able to drop it.

Had I condemned him for his actions I am sure I would have helped reinforce his problem. In a very real sense he was involved in this situation looking for self-acceptance. In giving him my acceptance, he was able to give up his problem.

Be trustworthy. How sad it is when a person trusts us with his innermost sins, struggles, or feelings and we betray him by telling somebody else. Sometimes we do this under the guise of "so-and-so needs our prayers." "He is involved in such-and-such," we piously say. "Will you please pray for him?" This can be an insidious form of gossip.

> If giving advice worked, there wouldn't be many
> problems left in the world.

No advice, please. Dr. Chuck Roost, an old friend, used to talk about people who are cursed with the affliction to give advice. It took some time for me to grasp what he meant. Giving advice, especially when it is neither asked for nor wanted, is a put-down. It implies that I know more than you. I am better qualified than you to tell you what you should do. Furthermore, if giving advice worked, there wouldn't be many problems left in the world. The trouble is, advice doesn't work. If I want to tell you how to run your life and make your decisions for you, that may make me feel important, but it keeps you over-dependent on me, and both of us immature. To help you see your options and come to your own decisions is considerably more growthful for both of us.

Another friend, Don Martin, phoned me one time. "Dick," he said, "I've got a big decision to make about my future employment. I need your advice. Could you drop in?"

"I don't have any idea what you should do," I replied, "but if you want to use me for a sounding board, I'll be happy to come over."

When I got to his place I asked Don, "What are your options?" He spelled them out clearly, and then I suggested, "Okay, Don, let's do a role play. I'll be you and you be me. If you were Dick, what would you tell Don to do?"

He then proceeded to tell himself what he needed to do. He advised himself and worked it out fine.

Another problem with seeking advice (not counsel) is that you can go to four different godly people and get four differing pieces of advice—so you know the advice is not of God. As we trust in Him, God will lead us to work out our decisions for ourselves. This is a part of maturity.

Be a Caring Person

Being a caring person is another very real way we can be Christ to others. We can do this in many different ways. The following are a few suggestions.

Weep with those who weep. Chuck Swindoll in his book *Killing Giants, Pulling Thorns*, tells about "a little girl who lost a playmate in death and one day reported to her family that she had gone to comfort the sorrowing mother.

" 'What did you say?' asked her father.

" 'Nothing,' she replied. 'I just climbed up on her lap and cried with her.' "[1]

What did Jesus do when His friend Lazarus died? He wept.

Rare is the friend who knows how to weep with those who weep.

Know when to be silent. In the same book, Chuck Swindoll tells about Joe Bayly, who lost three of his children. He quotes from Joe's book *The View from a Hearse.* Joe writes: "I was sitting, torn by grief. Someone came and talked to me of God's dealings, of why it happened, of hope beyond the grave. He talked constantly. He said things I knew were true.

"I was unmoved, except to wish he'd go away. He finally did.

"Another came and sat beside me. He didn't talk. He didn't ask me leading questions. He just sat beside me for an hour or more, listened when I said something, answered briefly, prayed simply, left.

"I was moved. I was comforted. I hated to see him go."[2]

Visit the suffering. James indicates that to visit people in their affliction is what pure religion is all about (Jas. 1:27). Two years ago my wife was struck down suddenly by a major stroke that left her in the hospital for months. She was also left with some residual effects. Not all, by any means, but some friends didn't know how to cope with our problem or know what to say. They withdrew from us.

This can be very painful to those who are hurting.

Be Sensitive to People

Another very important way to be Christ to people is not to give advice or a sermon but to be sensitive to their feelings, their suffering, and their needs.

At the time of my wife's crisis one person called several times. I shuddered each time, as I knew I would be in for another sermon. He made me feel worse. Another friend called to ask how I was feeling. I said that I wasn't coping very well and was feeling terribly discouraged and lonely.

"Are you in the Word, Dick?" he asked, and then advised, "You really need to be into the Word of God."

I felt hurt and replied, "Tell me, Bill, what do you do when you are hungry?"

When Elijah was so depressed that he wanted to die, God didn't say to him, "Rise and pray." He simply said, "Rise and eat." The one thing Elijah didn't need was a sermon or a Bible reading at that point of time. He needed a good feed. He was not only emotionally and spiritually exhausted, he was also physically exhausted.

Another person, Barbara—whom I'd never met before—came to me and said, "I just don't know what to say or do, but I want you to know that Mike and I really do care. This week we prayed and cried for you. We want to be a part of God's answer if we can. Please let us know if there is any way we can help."

Barb then said, "You need a hug," and gave me one.

I was deeply moved. I saw Christ in her.

Sensitive to feelings. I walked into the counseling center one evening and saw a young person standing in the kitchen looking very dejected and sad. I walked over to her, put my arm around her shoulder and said, "Hello, I have no idea who you are and I don't even know your name, but I do want you to know that God loves you dearly and I care deeply. Can I help you?"

Later that evening when the classes were over, this young person came to me and said, "You will never know how much what you did and said meant to me tonight. Thank you."

In these and similar situations, naturally we need to be sensitive to the Spirit of God, but there are times (perhaps many times) when we need to follow the dictates of our heart and express just what we are feeling to those around us whom we sense are in need.

Sensitive to suffering. People are adept at hiding their pain. As the old saying goes, "Many a smiling face hides an aching heart," and unless we develop a sensitivity to people's hurt, we all too often miss the opportunity to be Christ to them.

A few months ago I preached at a Sunday morning service in a small suburban church set in a very peaceful neighborhood. I remember looking out over the congregation that day. Everybody looked attractive in their Sunday attire, and I remember saying to myself, "These people don't need me. What would I have to say that could help them? They seem to have it all together."

After the service I stood at the entrance of the church and shook hands with everyone as they left. They were all friendly. They thanked me for coming.

However, one man I shook hands with was recently retired. Apparently he was very depressed. Three days later he committed suicide. I totally missed his despair and pain. I presumed I was not needed and failed to be Christ to that man that day.

An early American Quaker is credited with these words: "I shall pass through this world but once. Any good thing therefore, that I can do, or any kindness that I can show to any human being, let me do it now. Let me not defer it or neglect it, for I shall not pass this way again."

Sensitive to needs. People, being human, always have needs, especially for love and warmth. Nobody ever receives too much love, and many are suffering from emotional deprivation through a lack of love. To survive, people need love and attention, someone to talk to, a shoulder to cry on, and they need touching and hugging.

Take the single, widowed, or divorced woman (or man) for example. So often she is feeling lonely and isolated. She very much needs some hugging from those in the group. But in many of our churches we're afraid to do this, and sometimes even withdraw from her. Because we don't meet her needs we can force her to get her needs met from those who might use her or take advantage of her. But if she does sin, while she is responsible, so are those of us around her who have failed to reach out and help meet her needs for love and affection.

And what about the lonely teenagers around us?

Many come from unhappy homes and are starving for love and affection. If we in the church don't give them the love and hugging in the group, we force them to get it on the backseat of a car—and then condemn them when they get into trouble. But when we fail to meet their needs, their sin is also corporate. We, too, are responsible. We are so individualistic in the West that we often forget that, as Christians, we are all members of Christ's Body. We are one body. When one suffers, we all suffer (1 Cor. 12:26-27).

To tell a person who is starving for human warmth and touch that he needs to have his needs met in God, is exactly the same as saying, "God will provide your need" to a brother who is cold and hungry. James had something to say about this: "Suppose a brother or sister is without clothes and daily food. If one of you says to him, 'Go, I wish you well; keep warm and well fed,' but does nothing about his physical needs, what good is it? In the same way, faith by itself, if it is not accompanied by action, is dead" (Jas. 2:15-17).

And the need for touch is only one of a thousand needs all around us every day. One problem is that when our own needs are being met, we tend not to be sensitive to others' needs.

Being a part of God's answer is another practical way we can be Christ to others.

Be Available
There were times when Christ needed to be alone or just with His disciples or friends. But this was not all of the time. Much of the time He was available to those who truly needed Him. We too need to be avail-

"ARE YOU JESUS?"

able as a good neighbor and be willing to be a part of God's answer.

Be a neighbor. In the rush of modern life most of us are too busy, but even in the midst of a busy life we can let our neighbors know that when they need us, we are always available.

I'm not one for being in and out of my neighbor's home. Proverbs warns us about overdoing this type of thing (25:17). However, when we moved into the last community where we lived, in due course I assured my neighbors that I would want them to call on us if ever they were in need. Over the years, in the process of being neighborly, I found that appropriate times came when I was able to talk about my Christian faith without having to force it.

Be a part of God's answer. We cannot meet everybody's needs, but we can all meet some. There are times when I need to pray not only for a friend's needs but also to ask God if there is any way that I can be a part of the answer.

I recently met a young man who was very lonely. He was badly needing some social life. We agreed to pray together that God would provide his need. To make this possible he had a particular need that I was able to meet at that time. Not only did I pray but I was also able to be a part of the answer.

Being a part of God's answer is another practical way we can be Christ to others.

Be Loving

To be Christ to people, we need to be many things, but above all we need to be loving. Love has many facets. Let's look at just a few.

Be accepting. God hates sin because it destroys that which He loves—us. But He always loves the sinner. God never condones sin. But he never condemns the sinner who acknowledges his sin and puts his trust in Christ to save him from his sin (Rom. 8:1). Of the two kinds of sinners in Christ's day, whom did He prefer to mix with? The honest ones—those who admitted their weaknesses and didn't try to hide behind a religious facade. The dishonest sinners condemn themselves.

We tend to think of God as punishing sinners. But that isn't really so. Sinners punish themselves. The wages, or more, the consequences of sin are death— that is eternal separation from God (Rom. 6:23)— just like the wages or consequences of jumping off a high building are death. Because God loves the sinner He has provided a net of salvation into which fallen sinners can jump. Those who refuse to accept that net condemn *themselves* to eternal death, God doesn't.

God separates the sinner from his sins. He loves and accepts us all just as we are. That is hard for us to do, but we need to work towards it because we are all sinners—equally (Rom. 3:23).

Be empathetic. Empathy is to enter another person's world. It is to get under his skin to know not only what he is thinking but also what he is feeling, and to feel with him.

Empathy is experiencing another person's presence and his experiencing yours. It is an essential part of loving and being Christ to another.

Gerard Egan says that this presence or "this 'being with' depends ultimately on your ability to care about others, to move away from the self-centeredness to which we are all subject, and to experience another's experiencing."[3]

This is difficult to achieve because, as Huxley suggests, "We live together, we act on, and react to, one another; but always and in all circumstances we are by ourselves. The martyrs go hand in hand into the arena; they are crucified alone. Embraced, the lovers desperately try to fuse their insulated ecstacies into a single self-transcendence; in vain."[4]

Or as Egan explains further, "Accurate empathy at its fullest, as a way of relating instead of just a communication skill, is an attempt to penetrate this metaphysical aloneness of the other."[5]

Faul and Augsburger put it this way: "Simple presence is the most fundamental form of non-verbal recognition and communication between persons. It is the elemental language of relationship, the chief means of granting or withholding approval, recognition, and validation of others. Presence is the essence of caring and love."[6]

Presence is giving another person your full attention. It may not involve saying or doing very much. It is an awareness that the other person is with you. He is not shutting you out but is with you in an open, caring, accepting and loving presence. You sense and you feel his presence. It's the opposite of withdrawal.

> Giving another person your presence is a powerful way to communicate Christ.

In all close relationships, and especially in marriage, "the most common violence is bitter silence. To ignore another's presence, or to refuse to acknowledge his or her worth and significance, can be an invitation to die."[7]

Muriel James and Dorothy Jongeward add, "Ignoring and isolating people are well-known forms of punishment even for adults. Such punishment deprives persons of even minimal stroking and leads to intellectual, emotional, and physical deterioration."[8]

Giving another person your presence is a powerful way to communicate Christ. People join groups or come to church because they need friendship and fellowship. To give them our presence, and thereby penetrate their aloneness, is true fellowship. It is being Christ to someone in need.

And, incidently, true prayer and worship are based on the same principle. Do we give God our presence? Do we experience His?

Love unconditionally. A rich young ruler came to Jesus genuinely wanting to know how to inherit eternal life. Jesus could see that his priorities were all out of order, so He told him to give his money away and follow Him. Christ's advice hurt, as this young man was very wealthy. He chose not to follow Christ and went away sorrowful (Mark 10:17-22).

The beautiful thing was that even though Christ knew that this young ruler would not accept or follow Him, He loved him (v. 21). That's unconditional love.

Love that says, "I will give you my love if you believe the same as I do, if you do what I want you to do, if you conform to my image of what I think you should be, if you stay popular, remain beautiful, get good grades, don't cause any trouble," or whatever, isn't love at all. It's control.

Unconditional love involves not merely the heart. It is an act of the will. It says: I will love you no matter what—no matter what you do, what you become, what you believe, I will love you. I will accept you. I will make a commitment to you. I may not like what you are doing to yourself. I may not agree with you. I may not believe as you do, but I will accept you and will commit myself to you and your growth.

> Unconditional love is a commitment not only to Christ but also to people.

If you need kindness, I will give you kindness. If you need warmth, I will give you warmth. If you need hugging, I will give you hugging. If you need firmness or tough love, I will give you tough love. If you need me to confront you, I will confront you. Where you need freedom, I will give you freedom. I will in no way seek to control you, to dominate you, to manipulate you, or use you.

Unconditional love is a commitment not only to Christ but also to people—especially to the people we are seeking to win to Christ.

Do you know why some people, including our own children, do not come to Christ? Could it be because we do not love them unconditionally or have not made a commitment to their growth? Sometimes, instead of loving others to meet their needs, we love them to meet ours.

Give yourself. Forgive me for sharing this story with you, for when it comes to being Christ to others and growing in love, I have a long, long way to go. But I think I had one of the best compliments ever paid to me recently. I'd been away from home studying. I'd been feeling particularly lonely and homesick, was struggling with being a full-time student again and was going through some deep personal struggles. I had shared my struggles with Mike, a much younger student whom I had come to appreciate. One day he said to me, "Dick, I have learned more about Christ through you in the past couple of months than I have in the last couple of years."

I was rather taken aback and felt strongly that his comments were not justified. "Come on," I exclaimed, "you have to be kidding. How could that possibly be? I've really been feeling in the pits and have felt like throwing in the towel, and you say you've seen Christ in me!"

"It's just the fact that you're being yourself," Mike answered. "You're not trying to pretend that you don't have any struggles or weaknesses. You just share yourself as you are. In that I see Christ."

So often we're trying to be good to impress others with our goodness so that we'll be a "good testimony" for Christ. We don't do this and we don't do that. We won't go here and we won't go there (neither do the people in the cemetery—they're dead too). But people are never impressed with our goodness for goodness sake—especially if the goodness is only external acts and we never give ourselves. It's like the parent who does endless things for his child, provides everything he needs; he stuffs him with food but never gives himself. Then the parent wonders why the child rebels. "Look at all I've done for you," the parent moans laying on the guilt. "How could you treat me like this?" It's because the child never felt loved. The parent never gave himself. People feel loved only when we give them ourselves and our presence.

To be Christ and to communicate Him to others we need to be ourselves and give ourselves—to give the Christ in us. As the Apostle Paul wrote, "We loved you so much that we were delighted to share with you not only the gospel of God but *our lives as well*, because you had become so dear to us" (1 Thess. 2:8, *italics added*).

People outside the church don't want to hear what

the Bible says about Christ. They want to see *Him*, hear *Him*, and feel *Him* in us.

As Glenn Arnold puts it: "Show me. Don't tell me."

Sydney Carter feels the same way. His expression of this concept is captured on a poster I recently saw.

The Living Truth is what I long to see;
I cannot lean on what used to be.
So shut the Bible and show me how
the Christ you talk about is living now.[9]

Questions for Study

1. What is the difference between communicating a message about Christ and communicating Christ?

2. How can you be Christ to others? Think of the people you know (these are the ones you are to "witness" to first) and ask yourself how you can be (1) a friend, (2) a caring person, (3) sensitive, (4) available, and (5) loving to each one of them.

3. What are other ways you can be Christ to others?

4. What does it mean to give another person your presence? Think of your relationships. Do you give your loved ones, friends and personal contacts your presence?

5. When you are "being Christ" in your "Jerusalem"—your home and to your friends and acquaintances, how can you expand your field of influence to your own "Judea and Samaria, and to the ends of the earth"? Set some definite goals for following the Great Commission.

Notes

1. Charles R. Swindoll, *Killing Giants and Pulling Thorns*, (Portland, OR: Multnomah Press, 1979), pp. 39-40.
2. Ibid., p. 39.
3. Gerard Egan, *Interpersonal Living*, (Monterey, CA: Brooks/Cole Publishing Company, Inc., 1976), p. 137.
4. Ibid.
5. Ibid.
6. John Faul and David Augsburger, *Beyond Assertiveness*, (Waco, TX: Calibre Books, 1980), p. 41.
7. Ibid.
8. Muriel James and Dorothy Jongeward, *Born to Win*, (Reading, MA: Addison-Wesley Publishing Company, 1971), p. 52.
9. Sydney Carter, on a poster at Wheaton College.

Part II
Throw Away the Mold

Six

LOVE PEOPLE: USE PROGRAMS

If you were asked what you felt was the church's number one sin or weakness, what would you say?

Apathy? Being over-programmed? Too much secularism? Too much social gospel? Not enough social responsibility? Too worldly? Too other-worldly? Too liberal? Too conservative?

If I were asked this question I would say that I feel our major weakness is that we have become too program centered rather than being people centered. Or we have become too leader centered, too message centered, or even too "Bible" or "Christ" centered instead of being people centered—that is, in our ministry.

Before you jump to hasty conclusions and write me off as a heretic, I'd like to explain exactly what I mean.

In our relationship to God we certainly need to be Christ centered. He is the only way to God and in Him we live and move and have our being (John 14:6; Acts 17:28).

And in our beliefs, doctrine, theology, and manner of life we certainly need to be Bible centered. That is, in matters of faith and practice the Scriptures are our guide and our final voice of authority (2 Tim. 3:16-17).

However, in our ministry we need to be people centered if we are going to effectively communicate Christ's message and God's Word.

In actual *ministry* Jesus was never program centered, leader centered, message centered, Bible centered or God centered. He used programs such as sending out His disciples two by two. He was a leader Himself and used other leaders. He always had a simple but profound message. At appropriate times He quoted the Scriptures and was God Himself, clothed in human flesh. But in ministry He always started with the individual and ministered to his or her need. This is what made Him people centered.

Jesus loved people and used programs. He always discerned what the individual's need was and adjusted His program, message or ministry to meet that person's need—never the other way around.

In everyday life it is easy for us to unconsciously love things and use people instead of loving people and using things. It's the same in the church. Unless we make a conscious effort to put people first, we may unwittingly love our programs, our doctrine, our beliefs, and even the Bible more than we love people, and end up unhappily using people to support our programs and beliefs—a subtle but dangerous path to follow. Let's look at some of these dangers.

Program Centered

When I was a young pastor fresh out of college, I was enthusiastic, highly motivated, and genuinely wanted to see people come to Christ and have my church grow. People did come to Christ and the church did grow, and I thought I was on the ball. But I had at least one major problem. I was too program centered.

At the time I was somewhat deficient in understanding people, but I understood programs. I had been trained in programs. I had a program for just about every phase of the church life: for increased church and Sunday School attendance, for growth in the youth department, for missions, for evangelism, for visitation, for preaching, for teaching, for witnessing . . . all very good in and of themselves except for one thing: I started with the programs and not the people.

I didn't know it at the time, but I was heading for trouble. Eventually I began to dry up. Instead of starting with the people's needs and designing programs, ministry, teaching, etc., to fit into and meet their needs, I always started with the programs and tried to get people to fit into those programs. For some, the programs happened to meet their needs. But for many they didn't, and these people were left out.

Worse still, as I mentioned in an earlier chapter, I even quoted Bible verses to support my programs and get people to do what I wanted them to do. I have since returned to that church and apologized for my approach. If I were there today as pastor, I may still be using some of the same programs, but I would start with the people first, find out exactly what their needs were and design all programs, teaching, and preaching to meet their needs and not mine. This is what I mean by being people centered rather than being program centered.

The New Testament is all but silent on methodology and is remarkably free of programs.

Most of the time we just *drift into being program centered*. Because God blessed a certain program or method in the past, we tend to cling to that method religiously. However, because God blessed a program last century, last year, or even last week is no guarantee that it will be effective this week. I am certain that this is why the New Testament is all but silent on methodology and remarkably free of programs. Imagine what we would do if we knew exactly how the three thousand people made their decision to receive Christ on the day of Pentecost? Or what kind of "altar call" or "invitation" Peter gave that day? Fortunately we don't know or we'd be using this as another issue to cling to or argue over.

Speaking about invitations or altar calls, like many of our programs, "it may come as a surprise to many to discover that the altar call, like the Sunday School, is of recent origin. One may read thousands of pages of church history without discovering a reference to such a practice before the last century. It is, in fact, a unique development of American protestantism."[1]

I have been in several magnificent church buildings in Australia whose sanctuaries, resplendent with architecture of a former era, and seating anywhere from five hundred to fifteen hundred people, once packed to capacity, are now all but empty. As I stood and preached in one of these recently, I couldn't help but feel that the "glory had departed," but the people knew not why. Times changed. The people changed. But the programs remained the same. One of these churches died. Another is still struggling. A third is now striving to change its program to meet people's needs.

A further reason we can slip into being program

centered is *because of mixed motives*—a problem many of us struggle with.

> The moment we become program centered, we begin to lose our effectiveness and eventually will die.

I had one preacher friend who, from all outward appearances, was a very successful pastor. He had built a large and thriving church. He was working to make his Sunday School one of the top ten in North America in attendance. He had developed a large bus ministry, instituted a day-care center for preschoolers, and had built a church-sponsored grade school and high school.

But something strange happened. His father died and he had a breakdown. In counseling he discovered his mixed motives. As a child he had never received any meaningful approval from his father, and his drive to be successful and build a big church was an unconscious attempt to gain his father's approval. When his father died, his inner self knew that he could never get that approval. At that point he collapsed and went for help. Once he saw why he was driving himself so hard and setting up all those programs he was freed to get off his private merry-go-round and become more people centered.

Regardless of the reason, the moment we become program centered we begin to lose our effectiveness and eventually will die.

Leader Centered
As E. M. Bounds has reminded us, "God's methods are men." God doesn't bless programs or methods. He blesses people. And the church certainly

needs strong people—strong leaders.

However, one very real problem strong leaders struggle with is the need to be in control and for their ministry to revolve around them rather than around the people to whom they are ministering.

Management expert Peter Drucker believes that "one way or another all makers of men are demanding bosses."[2] He goes on to explain that all strong people have strong weaknesses. The key to make this type of man effective is to start with the person, find out what his strengths are, and put him in a position where he can make full use of his strengths. Never start with the job and make the man fit into the job or the program. Start with the man and make the job or the program fit into his strengths. This will automatically minimize and render harmless his weaknesses. This is being people centered in leadership.

Strong leaders therefore need to be sure that they don't use people to meet their own goals nor pressure them into the molds of their own programs. But rather they need to find out not only what they themselves do best, and major in that, but also what others do best and put them where they are best suited to make full use of their gifts and abilities. Doing this ensures that the organization or church doesn't revolve around and become over-dependent on him. This gives an organization a future.

Message Centered

Some preachers are so gifted that people flock to hear them. However, these men are the exception, especially in this day when at the turn of a knob people have all sorts of entertainment right in their own living rooms. Most of us preachers are made of much lesser stuff and need to major on speaking to people's needs and not build our ministry around our preaching, if we are to be effective communicators. This is not to say that we shouldn't work hard and do our utmost to be as good speakers, preachers, teachers or writers as we can possibly be. God expects this of us and people shouldn't or won't listen to us if we don't.

The important point though is to be people centered and not message centered. That is. we need to start our preparation with the needs of the audience in mind and not with our message or style of preaching.

One popular school of thought is convinced that if God is going to bring revival, He will do it not only through preaching, but specifically through a certain type of preaching. Who am I to disagree with the experts, but if revival comes I feel it will come only through national suffering which will cause people to become more open and honest with themselves, with each other, and with God—regardless of which style of preaching, if any preaching at all, ushers it in. Again I'd agree with E. M. Bounds. God blesses people, not methods.

Jesus wasn't method centered. He was people centered. He always started with the people's needs and made His methods fit their needs. Never the other way around.

Bible and Christ Centered

This is a touchy area. I may lose some friends and gain some enemies on this issue. How could any church be too Bible or too Christ centered? To say that we are Bible centered or Christ centered in our ministry sounds great, but it can be deceptive. By "preaching the Word" or by "preaching Christ" as we put it, we can believe that we are being faithful to

God, but at the same time fail to see our need to truly know and understand God, ourselves, and other people. And to be effective communicators, we need to know and understand ourselves and others as well as God.

Knowing God. In fact, we may know the Word of God, preach it and preach Christ, but that doesn't mean that we know God anymore than knowing the word of C. S. Lewis and preaching Lewis means that we know Lewis. Even if Lewis were still living and we knew his writings inside and out, that still wouldn't mean that we know him. To know C. S. Lewis we need to experience him. To know the Word of God is not to know God either. To know God, we need to experience Him. Learning *about* God is important, but if we're not careful, it can actually stop us getting to know *Him* personally. Furthermore, it can stop us getting to know ourselves and other people as well.

Knowing ourselves. For many years I was so busy studying God's Word and being involved in church programs I never took the time to get to know myself or understand other people. Instead of standing on the Word of God as I thought I was doing, I was actually hiding behind it; that is, hiding my true inner self which was very much repressed. While I was trying to be intellectually honest, I was being emotionally dishonest.

What I didn't realize was that intellectual honesty apart from emotional honesty is a myth. As long as I am not being honest with my inner self (the heart) and don't have a true picture of myself, I simply cannot have a true picture of God's Word either.

Or to put it another way, the interpretation of all truth, including God's truth, is as each person per-

IS THE BIBLE YOUR FOUNDATION OF MINISTRY
TO PEOPLE AND THEIR NEEDS OR IS IT THE
WHOLE BUILDING?

ceives it. Therefore, to the degree that I am untruthful with myself, I will distort God's truth and be blind to many of its personal applications.

Knowing people. To be an effective communicator, we need to understand not only ourselves but other people too. This is imperative. One is dependent on the other. We simply cannot know and understand others until we know and understand ourselves. We may know and understand the Bible from cover to cover. We may be a master of its original languages and may have a profound grasp of the meaning of every word and grammatical implication. But if we don't know and understand ourselves and other people we will unconsciously use the words of the Bible to control or manipulate other people.

The purpose of the Bible. Sometimes, too, instead of making the Word of God our foundation for ministering to people's needs, we make it the whole building. That is, instead of using God's Word as the base or foundation to reach out and minister to our communities and the wider world, we invest much of our time and energy studying, preaching, and teaching the Word, while people all around us—both inside and outside of the church—are hurting, are lonely, are in conflict with themselves and others, are sexually frustrated, have marriage problems, family problems, personal problems, etc., etc., and are desperately in need of Christ's healing and wholeness. Instead of struggling to be a healing agent, we're sitting around defending the Word of God. The best defense of God's Word is to put its principles to use.

To major on knowing the Bible as an end in itself is to be guilty of the sin of bibliolatry.

Others use the Word of God primarily to stop doing wrong acts but not as a basis for personal growth, wholeness, and getting actively involved in helping others grow.

Author Gerard Egan has an interesting word to say about these people. He writes, "Their relationships with others are not noticeably destructive, but neither are they growthful and engaging. They are bland. Their home lives are neutral—neither hotbeds of neurotic interaction nor centers of interpersonal stimulation. They profess certain religious values— that should draw them closer to their fellow human beings—but in practice these values are ritualistic and restraining, holding them back from doing wrong rather than impelling them to involve themselves as effective helpers in their communities."[3]

Sad to say, this is what can and does happen when we become "Bible centered" in our ministry rather than being people centered. And in so doing, Egan adds, "our growth is on a plateau, immobile, and we will inevitably become the victims of our own boredom."[4]

To major on knowing or teaching the Bible as an end in itself is to be guilty of the sin of bibliolatry. It is to miss the whole purpose of the gospel. The purpose of knowing God's Word is to motivate us to know God, to know ourselves, to know other people, and to minister to their needs—as Jesus did.

People Centered

One of the major differences between Jesus and the Pharisees was that Jesus was people centered and the Pharisees were program centered. Jesus loved people and used programs while the Pharisees loved programs and used people. This in turn made the Pharisees authoritarian, but they had no real authority. And while Jesus was never authoritarian, He always spoke with authority.

In fact, the Pharisees loved their doctrines, their external piety, their rules and regulations, and even the Scriptures more than they loved people. It was more important to them that Jesus kept the Sabbath than that He heal sick people on the Sabbath.

As a matter of fact, when Jesus healed the impotent man who had been crippled for thirty-eight years, the religious Jews persecuted Him and sought to kill Him "because Jesus was doing these things on the Sabbath" (John 5:16).

Can you imagine that? Loving their rules and keeping the letter of God's law rather than wanting a man to be made whole? It's hard to understand.

But sometimes we do it too. Perhaps not so blatantly, but we do it nevertheless in subtle ways. It's easy to miss the spirit of the law and replace it with the letter of the law and end up loving the law, the Bible, or a particular doctrine more than we love people.

Many a time I've been asked by supporters of our ministry about my doctrinal position. It's not that I'm against sharing it, but the emphasis is wrong—I've never been asked if I love and understand people. I've had my personal support dropped because I didn't have a doctrinal statement on certain cultural (not biblical) issues, or because I quoted somebody from an "unacceptable" denomination.

Doctrine and theology are important, but they are not the most important. Loving God, yourself, and your neighbor is the most important. Do these, Jesus said, and you will automatically fulfill the whole law of God (Matt. 22:40).

"Wherever Jesus went there was either a revival
or a revolution. Wherever I go, they serve tea."

Jesus loved people. Because of this He was committed to their healing and to their wholeness. But
this doesn't mean He was wishy-washy or weak. Let
us never think of Christ only as "Gentle Jesus meek
and mild," and confuse meekness with weakness.

As an English Bishop once said, "Wherever Jesus
went there was either a revival or a revolution. Wherever I go, they serve tea."

Jesus was a man of passion. He hated the abuse of
God's house so He threw out the money changers—
with a whip. He hated evil and sin, not because these
were opposed to His Word but because they were, and
are, damaging to human personality. But He always
loved sinners and was against anything that hurt
them, kept them in bondage, or hindered their
growth. And He was hated for His stand.

"In Jesus' case, we have the story of the holiest
man who ever lived, and yet it was the prostitutes
and lepers and thieves who adored Him, and the religious who hated His guts."[5] Why? Because He loved
ordinary people and was opposed to religious dogma
and programs that used people rather than helping
them to grow.

"People were offended with Jesus because he vio-
lated their understanding of religion and piety. The
religious of his day were particularly incensed that he
deliberately healed on the Sabbath .... They
accused him of being a drunkard, a glutton and having tacky taste in friends. As Gene Thomas is fond of
saying, 'Jesus was simply not your ideal Rotarian.' It
is a profound irony that the Son of God visited this

planet and one of the chief complaints against him was that he was not religious enough."[6]

In other words, Jesus was committed to people's growth and was strongly opposed to anything that stopped or hindered that growth.

In his book *The Gagging of God,* Gavin Reid, an English minister, talks about the "crisis of a non-communicating church in a non-communicative society."[7]

In the last two centuries, from the early 1700s to the early 1900s, for example, Great Britain experienced some profound movements of God. It was at that time the most influential missionary-sending country in the world and produced some of the world's leading men of God: John and Charles Wesley (1703-1791), William Carey (1761-1834), William Booth (1829-1912), Charles Spurgeon (1834-1892) to name but a few.

But the spiritual condition of Great Britain is vastly different today. Only a decade ago *Christian Life* reported that church attendance there had fallen to 2 percent of the population.[8]

Reid feels that a major reason for the failure of the church in England to communicate the gospel and effectively evangelize its own country was because the church failed to change its methods in changing times. In other words, they became bogged down in being program centered and consequently lost their effectiveness.

According to the seventh Earl of Shaftsbury, "The parochial system is, no doubt, a beautiful thing in theory, and is of great value in small rural districts; but in the large towns it is a mere shadow and a name."[9] And he said that over a hundred years ago.

"As fishers of men the churches can no longer

await the arrival of shoals into their carefully built reservoirs, and to plan church strategy on the assumption that uncommitted people are going to come to *meetings* in church halls is to invite frustration upon frustration."[10]

And as for us "to assume that non-attendance at church-controlled activities is evidence of godlessness and 'hardness of heart' shows a complete lack of understanding of and sympathy with the non-churchgoer."[11] People only keep coming to church if their needs are being met. If they are not, they eventually stop coming.

It would be very wise, therefore, for the church in North America, Canada, Australia, New Zealand and other lands to see what happened to church life in Great Britain in a relatively short period of time. From being a powerful spiritual force it dropped to a very small minority—2 percent—of the population attending church.

The same thing can happen in other lands and places as well.

Know Them to Reach Them

The effective Christian communicator is one who not only understands God and His Word, but also understands people and knows the needs of his audience. Whether he is speaking to one person or a thousand makes no difference. The principle remains the same. He makes the effort to know his audience primarily because he loves people and has their well-being in mind. He does not come with a preconceived program, nor does he stick rigidly to any particular program. He constantly keeps in touch with the felt and perceived needs of his audience and plans his program, his teaching, his preaching, and his individual witnessing to speak and minister to those needs.

If it is an individual you are seeking to minister to, spend time with him. Get to know him. Share yourself and *your* needs with him. Be real. Share your struggles as well as your victories. Be a friend to him. Be genuinely interested in him. Listen to him. Hear what he is saying beyond his words—through his nonverbal communication. *Ask* him what his deepest needs are. And then be Christ to him by seeking to help meet his needs.

If it is a group or class you are ministering to, try to get to know each member personally. Ask them what their needs are. Within the group, periodically have the members write down several of their pressing needs, numbering them in order of importance.

If it is a large group or congregation, always provide some means of receiving feedback to ensure that you are on target with your audience's felt needs. Place a suggestion box in a prominent place. Provide pen and paper and constantly encourage members to write out their comments, constructive criticisms, suggestions and specific needs.

Another excellent way to know your audience or congregation is to conduct an annual survey. The secular world realizes the importance of conducting regular surveys of magazine readers, radio and television audiences, voters, and so on, to ensure that all communications are on target. Can Christians and the church afford to do less? I think not.

If you want to effectively communicate Christ's message to your unchurched community, discover what their predominant needs are and then determine your program and strategy accordingly. Get to know your community by speaking to school principals and counselors, social workers and agencies, volunteer organizations, doctors, counseling center directors, and so on. Or pinpoint the specific needs of the community by conducting a formal survey.

A member of your group who has had training and experience in research can help conduct a survey of your congregation, community, magazine subscribers, or radio audience. Or you can receive help from organizations who specialize in conducting these types of surveys. See suggestions in Epilogue.

Regardless of your audience, always discover the felt needs of the various segments or groupings first—such as the elderly, singles, youth, young marrieds, working families, unemployed, etc. Then, when determining your specific strategies, always ensure that they minister to these segments with their specific needs. This is the difference between being people centered and program centered. It doesn't matter whether the strategies used are the spoken word, teaching, training, meeting social needs, cassettes, radio, television, or the printed word. Commence with the needs of the audience, then in Christ's name minister to those needs.

In my own organization we specialize in providing radio spots for local churches, in addition we provide leaflets, brochures, and magazines to help individuals, organizations, and churches communicate Christ's message to non-Christians. When churches ask me for suggestions of what literature titles to select, I constantly emphasize the need for them to determine the felt needs of their audience, and then select materials that speak directly to those needs. In some cases we will specifically prepare materials for a particular church or organization's needs. Samples of these radio spots and outreach literature materials can be obtained by writing ACTS International. (See Epilogue for addresses.)

When communicating Christ's message to the unchurched, every message and activity doesn't have to have John 3:16 tacked on the end of it. Actually, there was only one person Christ gave that message to. And every cup of cold water doesn't have to have Romans 3:23 engraved on the bottom. The important thing is that we minister to people's needs in Christ's name—whether the need is spiritual, emotional, or physical. To do this *is to communicate Christ.*

In other words, let us not be guilty of loving our programs and using people to boost them. But rather, in Christ's name let us love people and use our programs to meet their specific needs.

At that point of time when the church changes from being people centered in ministry to being program centered, it begins to slowly lose its effectiveness and, unless arrested, dies.

Questions for Study

1. Does your church set up programs and expect people to "fit in"? Read what Paul says about the "body of Christ," which is also your local church, in 1 Corinthians 12:14-20. What are your "spiritual gifts"? How are you using them in the Body of Christ to minister effectively? (For more about discovering your spiritual gifts read *Your Spiritual Gifts Can Help Your Church Grow* by C. Peter Wagner [Ventura, CA: Regal Books, 1979].)

2. Do you agree with the author that revival will come "only through national suffering which will cause people to become more open and honest with themselves, with each other, and with God"? Why or why not? Can you find biblical principles that sup-

port your view?

3. Differentiate between being program centered and people centered.

4. In ministry, what is the *beginning point* for a church to become program centered?

5. Jesus was people centered in His ministry. How does the church of today differ in its ministry from the way Jesus conducted His ministry? List some specific ways your church can become more like Christ, that is more people centered, in its ministry. As an individual, how can you become more people centered in the name of of your local church and in the name of Jesus Christ?

Notes
1. Joseph C. Aldrich, *Life-Style Evangelism* (Portland, OR: Multnomah Press, 1981), p. 118.
2. Peter F. Drucker, *The Effective Executive* (New York: Harper & Row Publishers, 1966), p. 75.
3. Gerard Egan, *Interpersonal Living* (Monterey, CA: Brooks/Cole Publishing Company, 1976), p. 11.
4. Ibid.
5. Rebecca Manley Pippert, *Out of the Saltshaker and Into the World* (Downers Grove, IL: Inter-Varsity Press, 1979), p. 39.
6. Ibid., p. 40.
7. Gavin Reid, *The Gagging of God* (London: Hodder and Stoughton, 1969), p. 26.
8. Dick Innes, "Is Today's Church Boring?" *Encounter*, April, 1972, p. 1.
9. Reid, *The Gagging of God*, p. 23.
10. Ibid., p. 25.
11. Ibid., p. 88.

Seven

ONE STEP AT A TIME

About the turn of the century, according to Dr. Jim Engel, author and professor at Wheaton College Graduate School, Julia Woodward went as a missionary to Ecuador. Here she worked for over a half century with a tribe of Quincha Indians. During this time she reduced the people's language into written form, taught the people to read and write, and began to translate the Scriptures into their language. However, in all this time and in spite of all her labors she saw less than a handful of people become Christians.[1]

But were her efforts in vain? Hardly. Having spent her entire working life with these people, Julia retired and was replaced by Mr. and Mrs. Henry Clawson who picked up the work where she left off. What happened in the next fifteen years seems astounding. Almost this entire tribe of some fifteen thousand Indians embraced the Christian faith and joined the church.

Which of these missionaries do you think did the

most effective work of evangelism? Julia Woodward or the Henry Clawsons?

If we were giving out rewards for faithful service I'm sure I would cast my vote for Julia Woodward. However, when it comes to evangelism, I would say that the Henry Clawsons and Julia Woodward were both equally effective.

People who have never heard the gospel, or those who have a low level of understanding the gospel, as a general rule do not come to Christ without preparation of mind and heart. For most, depending on their background and experience, raising their level of God-consciousness and gospel awareness is a process which takes place over a period of time.

This is clearly seen in the work of Julia Woodward and the Henry Clawsons. While it may not take fifty years for most people to understand and respond to the gospel, there are principles involved that apply to all spiritual development. What are some of these principles?

Continual Sowing

In the case of Woodward and Clawson, one sowed, the other reaped (see 1 Cor. 3:6-9), but both evangelized. Without all those years of faithful and effective sowing and cultivation—over fifty years of it—there would have been no effective reaping.

I have been involved in literature outreach, working in conjunction with the local church for a number of years, and I constantly wrestle with the problem where people not only want but actually expect to reap where there simply has not been adequate sowing, and oftentimes none.

We don't really have to be farmers to know that if we are going to see a continual harvest, there has to

be continual sowing of the seed along with much cultivation. And without trying to stretch the illustration too far, we all know that about the only things
that come up by themselves and don't need tending
are weeds.

> In selling it's the seventh call, on average, that
> gets results.

The major purpose of the organization to which I
belong (ACTS International) is to help the local
church bridge the gap between itself and the
unchurched community around it. We are doing this
by conducting seminars on communication theory
for effective teaching, preaching, and outreach, and
by providing literature and radio tools that speak
directly to the felt needs of contemporary people. In
each community there may be some who are ready for
harvesting, but this is only because somebody else
had already planted the seed and done the cultivating. A careful and continuing sowing is both a
neglected and urgently needed ministry in almost
every community. Unfortunately some churches
make only one or two brief contacts a year—and
some less than this—with the people of their community and expect to reap and—even pray for—an
encouraging harvest. This of course is not being realistic.

Regardless of their strategies, it is only the
churches that are doing continual sowing that are
seeing a continual harvest. One church in Sydney,
for example, has been using our literature to reach
out to its community continually over the past two
years. As a result it has made many positive contacts,
seen many visitors, witnessed a reversal of falling

attendance, and gained new members, some of whom have become very active church workers.

According to one sales philosophy, in selling it's the seventh call, on average, that gets results. That is, a person needs to be contacted a number of times before he is ready to make a decision to purchase a given item. If it takes this much effort to see a decision to purchase a material product, how much more sowing and cultivating will it take to see a person make a decision to commit his or her life to Jesus Christ—a total life-changing experience?

In one town where I lived for three years the local drugstore had a letter in my mailbox every month. They never missed. Guess which drugstore I went to when I had a need? Their continual seed-sowing paid off. The advertising world is very much aware of this principle. It never lets up.

The same principle holds true for the local church. For a continual harvest there is no way around the fact that there needs to be a continual sowing. And depending on the level of God-consciousness and gospel awareness in the community, it may take many years of careful and persistent sowing before there will be a continual harvest.

The need is to not get discouraged and give up too readily. Paul reminds us, "Therefore, since through God's mercy we have this ministry [of telling His Good News to others], we do not lose heart" (2 Cor. 4:1). Solomon adds some equally good advice: "Whoever watches the wind will not plant; whoever looks at the clouds will not reap . . . . Sow your seed in the morning, and . . . let not your hands be idle, for you do not know which will succeed, whether this or that, or whether both will do equally well" (Eccl. 11:4,6). Or as the *The Living Bible* expresses this passage, "If you wait for perfect conditions, you will never get anything done. Keep on sowing your seed, for you never know which will grow—perhaps it all will."

Meeting People Where They Are

Another reason Julia Woodward was successful in her ministry was that she met her people at their level of spiritual understanding and development and not at where she expected they ought to be. She had to start at the very bottom.

Jim Engel, who has had many years experience in both evangelism and communications, has, along with some of his students and colleagues, developed a Spiritual-Decision Process scale to illustrate how people are at different levels of gospel awareness and spiritual development. (See Fig. 2.)

In communicating the gospel, Engel's scale differentiates between God's role, the communicator's role, and man's response. God and the Holy Spirit's role is in the area of general revelation, conviction, regeneration and sanctification. The Christian communicator's role is to communicate God's message. He may speak, but not necessarily communicate. If he doesn't communicate, the Holy Spirit can't convict. He does this through proclamation, persuasion, follow-up, cultivation, his own way of life, and ministering to people's needs. And as man hears God's Word he responds in one way or another.

The minus side of the scale represents the nonbeliever. At minus eight he or she has an awareness of a Supreme Being but has no effective knowledge or understanding of the gospel. Zero represents the point at which a person actually makes a commitment to Christ and becomes a Christian. The plus side of the scale is for the Christian. It represents his

Eternity

+8	
+7	
+6	
+5	
+4	Post-decision evaluation, fellowship in the church, Christian growth and maturity, fruits and gifts of the Spirit, discipleship, etc.
+3	
+2	
+1	
0	Point of conversion or new birth
-1	Repentance and faith in Christ
-2	Decision to act
-3	Personal problem/need recognition
-4	
-5	
-6	Increased understanding of the gospel and its implications
-7	
-8	Belief in a Supreme Being but no effective understanding of the gospel

Figure 2
The Spiritual Decision Process[2]

or her spiritual growth and maturity. It includes his or her post-decision evaluation, joining a local body of believers, learning and behavioral growth, communion with God, use of spiritual gifts, discipleship and so on.

One of the major concepts for the Christian communicator to grasp is that a person is not ready to receive Christ, nor is he open to hearing the plan of salvation, until he or she is at the level of personal problem recognition, which is at minus three on the scale. This is because people do not make major changes in their lives unless they feel a strong need to do so.

The individual who is self-satisfied, who is "rich and has need of nothing" is rarely open to the gospel. Rich or poor, if he is contented with his life as it is, and his personal needs are being met, he isn't searching for answers to life's problems. He thus has no desire to change. He is like the hard or rocky soil in Christ's parable (Matt. 13:5). The good soil which is receptive to God's Word is where a person recognizes his problems and is inwardly searching for an answer to meet his needs. Only then is he open to the claims of Christ upon his life.

However, if a person is not at minus three, two, or one, and we present the plan of salvation to him, at best he'll just have a closed mind to what we're talking about, but at worst he may be turned off to the gospel altogether.

Say, for example, that you are not a Christian and are only at minus seven or six and I present the plan of salvation to you and try to get you to make a decision to receive Christ. I may even get you to pray to invite Christ into your life, but in the process cause you to spiritually abort later on. Or I may cause you to close your mind to any further presentations of the gospel.

It is therefore essential to understand where people are coming from when we seek to communicate Christ's message and reach them at their level of spiritual understanding and development. Depending on the Holy Spirit, we can ask people questions about their understanding of the gospel to determine their level of spiritual development.

Evangelism is a process not an event.

Seeing the Total Picture

Not only is it important to reach people at their level of spiritual development, but it is equally important to realize that helping a person move from minus eight to minus seven, or from minus seven to minus six, and so on, is just as much a part and as important a part of evangelism as moving a person from minus one to zero—his point of conversion. We usually call these lower steps pre-evangelism, but any step that brings a person closer to receiving Christ is a vital part of evangelism.

When Julia Woodward went to Ecuador, the people, at best, would have been at minus eight. They, like many people would no doubt have been aware of a Supreme Being, but certainly wouldn't have had any understanding of the gospel. It took many years to raise their level of God-consciousness and gospel awareness. However, every step was a very important and critical part of their evangelization. We need to free our minds completely of the concept that evangelism takes place only when a person makes his or her commitment to Christ; that is, moves from minus one to zero. Every action, every influence, every word that draws a person even a half-step closer to Christ is evangelism. In other words, evangelism is a process not an event.

In fact, most of our evangelistic efforts to those outside the church need to be directed to the lower end of the scale, because that is where the vast majority of non-Christians are.

One of the major weaknesses in many of our witnessing programs is that we tend to have a fixed or pat approach to everyone. We may vary our introductory remarks a little—sometimes—but we still have the same canned message. It's like the salesperson technique we mentioned in an earlier chapter. He's administering a program rather than ministering to a person.

How different was Christ's approach to people. He treated every person He contacted as a separate individual and, sensing where they were coming from, always spoke to and ministered to their specific needs.

For instance, there is only one recorded instance in the life and ministry of Christ where He said to anybody, "You must be born again" (John 3:7). This was to Nicodemus who was already a religious man and very much involved in the "church life" of his day. Nicodemus recognized his problem and came directly to Christ for an answer to his spiritual need. He was already at minus three and was ready for a direct salvation message.

While some people are obviously ready for a direct message of salvation, the vast majority of those outside the church aren't.

In non-Western countries 90 percent or more of the population will be at minus eight at best. They may have some concept of God through the evidence of creation and their conscience, as spoken of by Paul in his letter to the Roman Christians. But as Jim Engel and Wil Norton explain, "This is hardly a sufficient basis for a life-changing decision. A simple presentation of the plan of salvation, often containing several Scripture references, is likely to make little sense to a person who doesn't even know what the Bible is, let alone its claims about God, the nature of man, and the uniqueness of Jesus."[3]

And in Western countries where the level of God-consciousness is somewhat higher, many, if not most of those outside the church, are much closer to minus six or seven than they are to minus three. True, they may have an initial awareness of the gospel, but how many have any clear understanding of the fundamentals of the gospel? In countries like Great Britain, Australia, and New Zealand where the societies are quite secular, even though most people believe in God, there is little understanding of the gospel by non-Christians.

Even in North America where church attendance is much higher, the level of gospel awareness of those outside the church is still well below the minus three level where almost all evangelism begins.

Thank God for the many evangelistic crusades where thousands have recorded their decision for Christ. However, it has been said that many of those responding to the gospel in these crusades come from a church background which, like Nicodemus, would give them a higher level of gospel awareness.

Listen to most evangelistic messages in the church, on radio, or on television and you readily see that the message is directed primarily to those who are at the minus three or above level. Pick up any tract in the average tract rack and the message is almost always directed to those at the minus three or above level. Look at all the books in your Christian bookstore and here you will find that the vast body of literature is directed to those on the plus side of the scale. Some are directed to those between minus three and zero, and almost none are directed to those at minus eight to minus three, where the vast majority of the non-Christians are.

In Australia, compared to North America, there is very little Christian radio and television programming, except for Sunday mornings when almost all of the programs are put on by an overseas electronic church. To say nothing about the serious problem of cultural adaptability, one seriously wonders about the millions of dollars being expended to air messages in the name of evangelism which give little or no consideration to the level of gospel awareness or the felt needs of the vast majority of the listening audience.

Consequently there is an urgent need for preaching, teaching, literature, radio and television programs, and cassettes that are designed to reach the millions of people who fall below the minus three level on the spiritual decision scale. And as this ministry appears, let us not rush in and brand it liberal or give it some other negative title—such as being from the devil—before we carefully evaluate it, simply because it is different to what we ourselves are used to seeing, hearing, and doing. And conversely, let us be careful not to justify all that we are doing under the claim that we are being faithful to the preaching of God's Word. If we are not being heard, we may not be proclaiming God's Word even though we are quoting Scripture.

One Step at a Time

Another important factor to keep in mind when communicating the gospel is that in any decision process people move only one step at a time. Some move more quickly than others, but if we force people to move at our pace instead of their own, we may do more to drive them away from rather than closer to Christ.

Let's say, for example, that I am a devoted member of a false cult called the Church of the Roman Centurian and I am wanting to make you a convert. You've heard about my church before, but you don't know too much about it so you're naturally suspicious and have your barriers up, but you do give me a hearing. Imagine if I try to move you on a similar scale from minus eight to zero in one or two presentations and even ask or pressure you to make a decision to commit yourself right now without delay to become a Roman Centurian. How will you react? In all probability you'll back right off and may close your mind completely to my church and any further presentation from me or any other member of my group.

There is a point up to which you are willing to give me a hearing, but the moment I try to push or persuade you beyond that point, you will close your mind. The mind is like the eye, the moment a foreign object tries to enter, it closes—tightly. If I try to put a new or a threatening idea into your mind too quickly, it also closes—tightly. Just realize how difficult it is to try and persuade a Baptist to become a Presbyterian or an Episcopalian a Baptist, let alone try and convert you to change your entire system of beliefs and values overnight.

As Griffin explains, "Every man is tolerant only up to a point. There's a range of opinion on either side of his position that he'll at least consider. Psychologists call this region the 'latitude of acceptance.' When he hears a message that falls within these limits, there's a good chance he'll be swayed by the appeal. Outside these limits lies his 'latitude of rejection.' Ideas within these areas will strike him as 'far out,' and he'll automatically reject them. In fact, they may even trigger [the] boomerang effect and drive him farther away . . . . In other words, persuasion—like Christian growth—is a gradual process."[4]

As we will see in the next chapter, people very quickly close their minds to anything that threatens their existing beliefs, their strongly held attitudes and values, their self-esteem or their personal lifestyle.

Therefore, if we want to convert others to our Christian faith, we will attempt to move their thinking only one step at a time. Author James Jauncey reminds us that "just buttonholing a stranger, witnessing to him and pressing for a decision will likely do more harm than good. Most responsible people react negatively and often quite violently to this kind of assault."[5] This type of approach shows not only a lack of respect for an individual's personal dignity, but also a fundamental lack of understanding of where he or she is in terms of his/her own spiritual decision process.

While it is good to rejoice over those who do come to Christ under our ministry, may we be equally sensitive to, aware of, and grieve over those we actually hinder or stop from coming to Christ. When we push people we can be sure we are "witnessing" out of our own need to quiet the rumblings of our false guilt or some other negative motive, and not ministering to meet the other person's need. And while we may see some come to Christ, we may never see the many we turn from Him.

To raise the level of God-consciousness and gospel awareness in a person's mind takes (1) continual sowing, (2) an understanding of where the person is coming from in terms of his or her own spiritual development, (3) a realization that evangelism is a process rather than an event, (4) an appreciation of the fact that each person needs treating as a separate individual, and (5) the knowledge that people grow only one step at a time.

But how do you determine where an individual, or where the members of a class, congregation, or community are in terms of their spiritual decision process? It isn't always easy, but once again the answer is in getting to know your audience by asking questions and, in the appropriate situations, conducting surveys.

What is a person's attitude towards God's Word? What does he know about Christ? In his opinion, who is Jesus Christ? What does Christmas and Easter mean to him? Why did Christ come, anyhow? What is sin? How can a person inherit eternal life? Is forgiveness of sin important? How can a person obtain forgiveness? Is there life after death? What kind of a relationship does he have with Jesus Christ? Who is the Holy Spirit? What does it mean to be born again? What does it mean to live in harmony with the will of God? Does God hold man accountable for his life and behavior? What is Christian love? What are the fruits of the Holy Spirit? The gifts of the Spirit?

These are the types of questions which, if asked appropriately, can help determine a person's level of gospel awareness and spiritual development. Naturally, they need to be asked tactfully and graciously, either informally or through more formal survey questionnaires. It goes without saying that the sensitive Christian communicator will also be dependent on insights from the Holy Spirit in coming to an understanding of a person's needs and in the determining of his or her spiritual development.

With a sound knowledge of your audience you can target both the approach and substance of your message and ministry. Without it you are shooting in the dark. Now and then you'll score, but how much better to be on target with your ministry most—if not all—of the time.

Questions for Study

1. As much as you can, make a list of the positive, effective ways in which your church has "prepared the soil" for sowing the gospel. What other ways do you think your church could employ?

2. If a church is going to see a continual harvest, what is required? Why is this essential?

3. The author says that the church needs to meet people "where they are." Looking at the spiritual decision scale (Fig. 2), where are the unreached people in spiritual development in your immediate church community? Where are you? the members of your family? the neighbors around you? See the questions the author asks to help you in your determination. List other ways you might be able to determine the level of a person's spiritual development.

4. What does much of today's evangelism (through personal witnessing, preaching, teaching, literature, the mass media) presume when seeking to proclaim the gospel to unbelievers in terms of their level of spiritual development?

5. To how many people did Christ say to: "You must be born again?" Where was Nicodemus on the spiritual decision scale? What was his background? What about the many others Christ ministered to, at what level of spiritual development were they?

6. What does the author mean when he says evangelism is a process not an event?

7. How do you feel about using a "canned" or standard approach to witnessing with every non-Christian you meet? When might a standard approach be helpful? When not?

8. Ask yourself and the people in your group how they came to Christ. What were the processes and influences that eventually brought you to Christ? Was your salvation an event or was it a process? When and how did this process commence? How long did it take? How do your answers apply to your witnessing to others?

Notes

1. James F. Engel, "Audience Psychology and Behavior," a lecture delivered at Wheaton College Graduate School, February, 1977.
2. Inverted and adapted from the Engel Spiritual-Decision Process model. For a more detailed version and fuller treatment see James F. Engel and H. Wilbert Norton, *What's Gone Wrong with the Harvest*, (Grand Rapids: Zondervan Publishing House, 1975), p. 45.
3. James F. Engel and H. Wilbert Norton, *What's Gone Wrong with the Harvest*, (Grand Rapids: Zondervan Publishing House, 1975), p. 47.
4. Emory A. Griffin, *The Mind Changers*, (Wheaton, IL: Tyndale House Publishers, 1976), pp. 138-139.
5. James Jauncey, *Psychology for Successful Evangelism*, (Chicago: Moody Press, 1972), p. 123.

Eight

OPENING CLOSED MINDS

"Hey, Dad, what do you think of that?" asked my teenage son as I was driving him to school one morning recently.

"What do you mean?" I queried. "What do I think of what?" I didn't have the faintest idea what he was talking about.

"That advertisement on the radio," he replied rather surprised.

"I just didn't hear it," was all I could say. "What was it about?"

The radio was at a reasonable volume. My ears were only inches away from the speakers, but I didn't hear one word the announcer said.

I'm sure you can readily identify with this type of experience. How often have you spoken to your husband, your wife, or your children—they were right there in the same room—but they didn't hear a word you said? Or how often have our wives, husbands, or children spoken to us and we were completely oblivious to what they said? Too often, I'm afraid. When I

PEOPLE SEE WHAT THEY WANT TO SEE.

talk to my wife and she doesn't hear me, I answer myself out loud. She gets the message. When my three-year-old talks to me and I don't hear him, he grabs my face, turns it around to face him and says in no uncertain tone, "Dad! I'm talking to you." Bless him.

Why do we tune out? Because we all have what the communicators call a *God-given filter system.* This is a kind of survival or defense mechanism in our mind which processes all incoming stimuli, blocks out all unwanted messages, and allows through only what we want to hear. Unconsciously, we choose to see and hear only what we want to see and hear.

In this day and age we are bombarded with so many incoming messages from newspapers, magazines, fliers, brochures, signboards, billboards, storefronts, posters, leaflets, bumper stickers, bulletins, radio, television, breakfast food boxes, the mail, school, church, work, friends, other people . . . that it is absolutely impossible to take them all in. The mind would literally boggle if it tried to process all this stimuli. But it can't, so it filters out all the unwanted messages.

We simply cannot escape the fact that people see and hear only what they want to see and hear. This is one of the most important factors to come to grips with in the whole area of effective communication. It's like the missionary in India. He didn't see any tigers and the hunter didn't see any missionaries. People see what they're looking for and close their minds to anything they don't want to see or hear.

How then do we overcome this problem? If people close their minds to messages they don't want to hear, how do we reach them for God?

To do this, the effective communicator will accept

the fact that every person has a filter which processes all incoming messages all of the time. He will seek to understand how this process operates. He will appreciate that the only way to open closed minds is by meeting people at their point of felt need. He will realize the importance of meeting felt needs before even attempting to meet real needs. And he will understand how people make a decision to act or change their way of life.

Filters Are a Fact of Life

It wasn't unusual for me to not hear the radio advertisement my son asked me about. It would have been unusual if I had heard it and paid any attention to it. Just think of all the radio and television commercials you hear and see. How many do you actually hear and remember?

Jim Engel says that "on the average, this is what happens: Out of every one hundred people who are actually exposed to a television commercial,

"Thirty actually attend to its content; that is they know what is being said;

"Fifteen understand the content (one half of those who attend to it initially);

"And only five retain its content in active memory twenty four hours later.

"This is a graphic illustration of how the human perceptual filter selectively screens incoming information. These kinds of effects are not confined to the commercial world. There are thousands of published and unpublished studies documenting selective screening in all phases of life."[1]

This principle applies to all communications—including Christian communications. It needs to be accepted and appreciated by any Christian who seriously wants to share God's message with others, whether on a one-to-one basis, in teaching a class, leading a group, preaching a sermon, writing a book or magazine article, or presenting a message via the mass media such as radio, television, and newspapers.

As individual witnesses, speakers, teachers, or writers, we only deceive ourselves if we think that people are waiting to hear what we have to say or write.

Eighteen years ago I had just completed several years of training and preparation for Christian ministry. I was filled with enthusiasm and vision and loved to preach. What a shock it was to discover in my very first pastorate that not only was the local community not interested in hearing what I had to say but neither were some of my own members. I had learned a lot about many things but I did not know the art of effective communication.

> Because we have sent out a message is no guarantee that we have communicated.

Let's be honest, how often do you and I tune out public speakers, teachers, and preachers? And of all the printed material that passes through our hands, how much gets thrown aside—unread? The sooner we learn that people hear only what they want to hear, the sooner we can learn how to become effective communicators.

Just because we have sent out a message is no guarantee that we have communicated. Only if the message is heard, attended to, understood, and acted upon, have we actually communicated. And only if the message is comprehended as we intended it to be

SELECTIVE DISTORTION

have we communicated effectively.

Because we have read or proclaimed even the Word of God is no guarantee that our message will be heard. The Holy Spirit cannot convict a person if that person hasn't heard or attended to the message. Effective communication involves much more than proclaiming Bible passages.

The classic Bible reference used to justify much of our witnessing and proclamation is Isaiah 55:11, which says that God's Word will not return to Him void. I have heard it quoted many times. I'm sure you have too. I have been guilty of quoting it, or rather misquoting it, many times myself. Only a few weeks ago, in an adult class where we were discussing this subject of communication, I was again challenged with this Scripture verse. "All we've got to do is preach the Word and God will do the rest. He has promised His Word will not return to Him void," one man stated with conviction.

"The problem is," I explained, "this Scripture doesn't actually say what many of us have come to believe it says."

"What does it mean?" he asked.

According to Engel this passage "makes reference to the great promises God has given Israel, especially those to be fulfilled after the return of the Messiah. It asserts that God stands behind His covenants, and the purpose was to give comfort."[2] In other words, God was saying to Israel, "I am making you this promise. And I never break my promises." It had nothing to do with proclaiming God's Word.

For years as a teenager I stood on a street corner every Sunday evening helping to proclaim "God's Word" through a loudspeaker, without any consideration of the audience's needs or interest. Nobody gathered around to listen to us, but the justification always was, "God's Word will not return to Him void." I'm not saying that we shouldn't proclaim God's message from a street corner. On some street corners this is still appropriate, on others it isn't. What I am saying is this: Preaching God's written Word, as we will see, is not necessarily proclaiming God's message. Enthusiasm does not make an approach valid and "zeal without knowledge" (see Rom. 10:2) can actually drive people away from Christ.

Unless we speak to the needs of our audience, we don't stand a chance of gaining a hearing.

This principle of filtering out unwanted messages was applicable not only in Christ's day but is even more applicable in our day. This is because of the ever increasing amount of incoming stimuli that we are all faced with, to say nothing of the continuing explosion of the world's body of knowledge which is doubling every five years. We simply cannot begin to contend with it all. By the time many university textbooks are written and published, they are already out of date. Even the most brilliant minds can only receive and process a limited amount of the messages that are vying for the mind's attention.

Another challenge to the Christian communicator in his attempt to gain the attention of people's minds is the fact that the older generation was trained to learn primarily through the ear gate, while the younger generation has been trained more to learn through the eye gate. Today's communicators need to use both methods. Furthermore, living in an educated and enlightened society, the average person can take in 700 words per minute, while the average speaker can give out only 120. This means that almost sixth-sevenths of the average speaker's time is lost time. If a listener's mind begins to wander it is difficult to regain his attention.[3]

Therefore, unless we're speaking to the needs of our audience we don't stand a chance of gaining a hearing. Our messages will be filtered out.

Information Processing

According to specialists in market research and communication theory, in processing all incoming information, people exercise what is known as selective exposure, selective attention, selective comprehension, selective perception, selective distortion, and selective retention.[4]

Selective exposure. Because people see and hear only what they want to see and hear, they tend to expose themselves only to messages that strengthen their present beliefs and attitudes, and avoid any messages they perceive to be irrelevant to their needs or threatening to their personal views, opinions, or convictions.

The evidence shows that more often than not a person will avoid a message he needs to hear while the same message will be listened to by those who don't need it but already believe it. In one study, for example, there was an interesting reaction to articles pointing out the connection between smoking and lung cancer. "Data showed that 67 percent of the nonsmokers claimed high readership of the articles, versus only 44 percent of the smokers."[5]

This principle is also demonstrated by the average gospel service in churches. Those who expose themselves to the message are mostly believers. This helps strengthen their existing beliefs, while those who need to hear it generally avoid it.

Many authorities will confirm that people self-censor or filter out messages that attack their beliefs and practices; that they will actively expose themselves to communications that strengthen their existing beliefs and practices; and will especially do the latter if their beliefs have been challenged or attacked.[6]

This of course poses a challenge to the Christian communicator. He needs to be aware of the fact that if people don't want to hear his message they will either avoid him or close their minds to what he has to say.

Selective attention. Kenneth E. Anderson, in his book *Introduction to Communication Theory and Practice*, says that "attention is a mental process by which a stimulus or a set of stimuli becomes distinct in consciousness while other stimuli tend to disappear."[7]

In other words, once a person has been exposed to a message he then either consciously or unconsciously (mostly unconsciously) makes a choice to attend or to not attend to that message. For example, if I call my boys to come and help clean out the garage on a hot day, they may show a totally different reaction to my calling them to come and have an ice cream and a cold drink.

We are all basically the same. We hear what we want to hear and filter out the rest.

> People can distort a message to say even the opposite.

Selective comprehension. This is similar to selective perception. Because a message has been initially attended to and accepted as being pertinent is no guarantee that it will be fully comprehended or perceived correctly.

For instance, "Have you ever seen a player argue with an umpire's decision in an important situation even when it was obvious to everyone else that the call was correct? The player *wants* the call to go the other way so badly that he might actually have perceived it differently from the umpire. I remember one case where a player even swore to his teammates that a called third strike was a ball. Later, when he was shown a videotape of the pitch, which was right down the middle, he couldn't believe it. He wanted it to be a ball so badly that he had *actually* perceived it to be a ball."[8]

Selective distortion. Not only can people see in a message what they want to see, but they can also distort a message to say even the opposite.

If, for instance, a person has a very poor self-concept, he will have a distorted filter that has a tendency to negate other people's words. If someone gives him a genuine compliment he may misconstrue this and see it as a form of manipulation. Because he doesn't believe in himself he can't accept that other's belief in him either. To match his feelings he distorts their messages.

Selective retention. Memory is also known to be highly selective. Not everything that is heard and understood will be committed to long-term memory. The most difficult things to remember are those things that are not pertinent to our particular needs and interests, or those things that threaten our lifestyle or beliefs.

As I said before, the mind is like the eye. The moment a foreign object threatens to intrude, the eye closes. So does the mind. It will close to anything that threatens a person's self-esteem, his personal life-style, his strongly held attitudes, values, and beliefs, and to anything that is not relevant to his felt or perceived needs.

As Myers and Reynolds say, "An idea, object, or event tends *not even to enter* the conscious mental stream unless it conforms reasonably well, not only with the things we have come to expect in our culture and society, but also with our own personal interests, goals, and objectives of the moment. If it does not, it tends to be overlooked, ignored, forgotten immediately, or otherwise rejected; as far as our conscious mind is concerned, it simply doesn't exist."[9]

Selective exposure shows that people will only be open to messages they wish to receive.

Selective attention shows that people hear only what they want to hear.

Selective comprehension or perception shows that people will perceive things the way they want to see them.

Selective distortion shows how people may change messages to match their self-concept.

And selective retention shows that people remember only what they want to remember.

Everything else is filtered out.

The Key to Opening Closed Minds

The mental filter is a God-given protective device. A person cannot even begin to process all the constant barrage of stimuli that comes to him, so he filters or screens out what he perceives to be irrelevant or what he doesn't want to hear. (See Fig. 3.) God knew that this would cause His message to be filtered out too. Therefore, if God wants people to hear His message there must be a way through the filter sys-

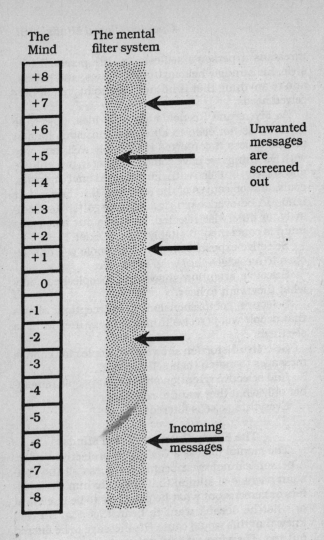

Figure 3
The God-Given Filter System

tem. There must be a key to open a person's mind and heart to God.

And there is. I believe that Jesus held it. Without exception, whenever He ministered to individuals in the New Testament He always reached them at their point of felt need. Jesus, being the Master Psychologist par excellence, fully understood people, knew their strongest need, and knew that the only way to gain a hearing was to reach them at their point of felt need. However, He didn't do this merely to get people to listen to Him and gain converts. He ministered to and met people's felt needs because He loved them. Jesus' goal was to make people whole, not just save their souls. To miss this is to miss the whole point of the gospel. But the starting point was always the individual's felt needs, and that is the key for gaining a hearing with any audience.

In the course of the past ten years I have driven down a particular road hundreds of times on my way to and from my office. There are at least two tile shops on this road, but for several years, even though I had driven past them hundreds of times, I had never seen them and didn't know they existed.

Then I began building my own home. When I got to the bathroom I had a felt need—tiles. As soon as I had that felt need I began to search for an answer to that need and found those two shops and several other tile shops almost immediately.

That's the way the mind works. When we have a felt need we seek a solution to meet that need, and our minds become open to all possibilities.

Gearing your message to the felt needs of any audience is the key to unlocking closed filters.

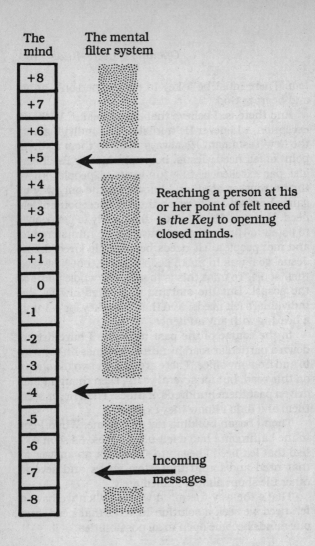

The mind

+8
+7
+6
+5
+4
+3
+2
+1
0
-1
-2
-3
-4
-5
-6
-7
-8

The mental filter system

Reaching a person at his or her point of felt need is *the Key* to opening closed minds.

Incoming messages

Figure 4
The Key to Opening Closed Minds

Think of yourself sitting in church. You can be looking directly at the preacher but your mind may be a million miles away. But let him start talking about one of your felt needs (e.g. love, sex, marriage relationships, teenage tangles, or whatever) and you'll be all ears.

The secret then to gaining an audience's attention and effectively communicating Christ's message is to identify with the felt needs of the audience and target your message to meet those needs. This is the only known way to open closed minds. (See Fig. 4.) Gearing your message to the felt needs of any audience is the key to unlocking closed filters. In fact, extensive research and documentation confirms that "people will not listen to the gospel message and respond unless it speaks to felt needs."[10]

Felt Needs Versus Real Needs

One problem many Christians struggle with is that they feel we need to minister to a person's real needs, which they usually interpret as being a spiritual need. This is to ignore the fact that God is interested not only in a person's spiritual life, but in his total person (Jas. 2:14-17). It also fails to understand that the felt needs or perceived needs are at the conscious level of a person's mind while his real needs—spiritual or otherwise—are usually at the subconscious level.

Therefore, the way to reach the real needs, whatever they are, is through the felt needs. It is the felt needs that lead to the real needs. (See Fig. 5.) As the conscious felt needs are faced and met, other needs will rise to the level of awareness and in turn become felt needs. As these are faced and met, eventually and spiritual and other real needs will surface to con-

The Mind

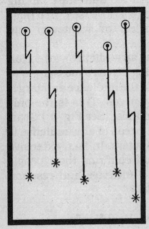

⊙ Felt needs are at the conscious level of the mind

∗ Real needs are often at the subconscious level of the mind

Figure 5
Felt needs lead to real needs

sciousness and in turn become felt needs. Only then can they be dealt with and met.

To ignore a person's felt needs and aim at other needs is a surefire way to guarantee that his mind will close and remain closed to our message. On the other hand, to understand and identify with a person's felt and perceived needs is a surefire way to guarantee that his mind will be open to what we have to say and will remain open as long as we offer hope to meet his needs. If he senses that we don't have the answers to his needs, his mind will close again to us and he will look elsewhere for a solution to his needs and problems.

The Decision Process

Extensive research has also shown that people go through a basic process in arriving at a decision to act. Whether this decision is to stop smoking, buy a new car or house, or change job or way of life makes no difference. The steps are the same. The effective communicator needs to understand and follow this process.

This process is seen in Figure 6 and is based on the Engel, Blackwell and Kollat model of motivational change.[11]

Identification of felt needs. As has already been seen, identification of the felt needs of the audience or individual, and tapping into that need, is the very first step and starting point for all effective communication. This and this alone is the key for opening closed minds and for getting through a person's mental filter system. It is also the starting point of the whole decision process.

Problem recognition on the part of the hearer or audience is the second step in the decision process. Until a person recognizes or has a felt need to change, there isn't any motivation or desire to change. This recognition of a need to change is called problem recognition.

People change only when they recognize and feel their need to do so.

Knowledge alone is not sufficient to cause a person to want to change his or her life. This is why doctrine, theology, and even Bible teaching in and of themselves do not change people's lives. This is also why knowledge about the dangers of smoking and risk of lung cancer doesn't stop millions of people from smoking. People change and grow only if they

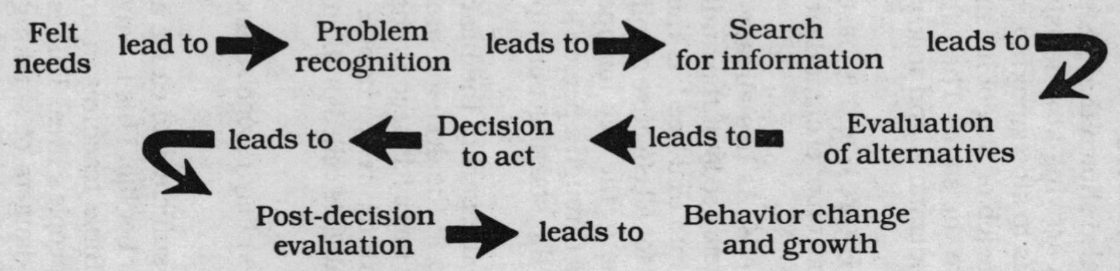

Felt needs lead to Problem recognition leads to Search for information leads to Evaluation of alternatives leads to

Decision to act leads to

Post-decision evaluation leads to

Behavior change and growth

Figure 6
The Decision Process

are hurting sufficiently and are uncomfortable enough with their present situation to want to change.

Pain is the great motivator. What is it that gets a person to the dentist quicker than anything else? Obviously, a toothache. A mild toothache will get him there in reasonable time. But a throbbing one will get him there immediately. Thus, the greater the discomfort a person has—the stronger his felt need and problem recognition—the greater will be his desire to find help and change.

The effective communicator will realize that he cannot change anyone. In fact, the only person he can change is himself. It is true that as he changes, those around him will tend to change also, but only because they want to change. To change, people have got to want to change and they want to change only when they recognize and *feel* their need to do so.

A search for information is the third step in the decision process. When an individual's personal beliefs, values or way of life no longer satisfy or meet his needs, his mind becomes open to change and he begins to search for answers and solutions to meet his needs and solve his problems.

It happens like this. If a person's lawn mower, washing machine or vacuum cleaner breaks down, he has an immediate felt need. He recognizes his problem and begins to look for a repairman to meet his need. As long as this equipment is working okay he has no interest in looking for help.

The same is true in all areas of life. If a person doesn't have a felt need for change he will not be looking for solutions to problems he doesn't recognize. This is why it is so difficult, if not impossible, to communicate the gospel to the self-satisfied and to those

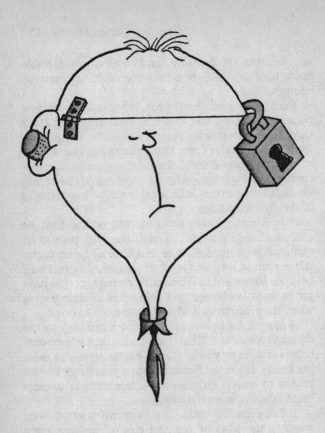

The key to opening closed minds

"who are rich and have need of nothing" (see Rev. 3:17). These are the "non-responsive soil" and are not white unto harvest.

Evaluation of alternatives. Once an individual recognizes his problem, his mind becomes open and he searches for the information he needs to resolve his problem. In his search he looks at various alternatives which promise to meet his need, and after evaluation of these alternatives he chooses the solution which he feels will best meet his need.

Decision to act. After the evaluation of the alternatives, then comes the decision to act or not to act.

One family I know about left their mainline denominational church to join what many would consider to be a false cult church. The reason for making this change was not any consideration of truth, but a consideration of needs. This family felt their family needs were not being met in their own church while the other church offered a program that would meet these needs.

This family had a strong felt need. They recognized their problem which opened their minds to change. They looked for answers to solve their problem. They evaluated the alternatives. Then they decided to act. They changed churches.

Post-decision evaluation. Immediately following a person's decision to act, comes his post-decision evaluation. "Did I make the right decision? Did I do the right thing? Is this what I really wanted?" he asks himself. If his needs begin to be met he will feel he has made the right decision. If not, he is likely to reverse his decision and start the whole process over again until he finds a way to meet or handle his needs.

Behavior change and growth. For the Christian,

once he has confirmed in his mind that he has made the right decision to receive Christ, his level of commitment or the reality of his decision will be seen in his actions, his way of life, and his growth.

When one set of needs is met, then a new set of needs is felt. Once again he looks for solutions, chooses and evaluates the various alternatives, and acts on the choices he makes. As this process is repeated, he grows. If the process ceases, he ceases to grow. These steps, of course, are not conscious, but they happen nevertheless. The effective communicator will realize this.

As much as we would like to think that people go to church to search for God and truth, or to hear us preach or teach, it just isn't so. They go to have their needs met. Even if the need is spiritual, people don't search for God for God's sake. They search for Him for their sake—to have their need for God met or to have their inner "God-shaped vacuum" filled. People also go to church to have all sorts of other needs met: friendship, fellowship, warmth, love, understanding, acceptance, a sense of belonging and many other personal needs.

And even if people did come to church to hear me preach, it wouldn't really be to hear me preach at all. It would be because, for some reason, my preaching happens to meet a need in them. Some of us have a need to preach, to teach, to speak, to write—a need to be heard; and that's perfectly acceptable so long as we recognize that others have needs too. Only as we speak to and minister to those felt needs can we be successful communicators and ministers.

Speaking to people's felt needs is *the* key to opening closed minds and effectively communicating the gospel. And meeting those needs is the whole purpose of the gospel. Only as people recognize their needs and problems do they become open and respond to the gospel.

> Only when a nation has a strong enough felt need does its people turn to God and be open for revival.

Consider the countries where God is moving in a profound way today—countries where many thousands have and are continuing to turn to Christ: Latin America, Indonesia, South Korea, Africa and Bangladesh. They all have one common denominator—suffering. They have been torn apart or disrupted by political upheaval, war, bloodshed, hunger, famine, and so on.

Their problems have upset their way of life, their values, their beliefs, and their philosophies of life. They have suffered greatly, become very unsettled, and had strong felt needs for change. This is what has made them open to looking for solutions, and they have turned to Christ and the Christian way of life in order to have their needs met. It is their suffering that has made them "white unto harvest."

When we pray for revival in our lands, we often don't realize for what we are praying. Without national upheaval there isn't too much hope for revival. Only when a nation has a strong enough felt need does its people turn to God and become open for revival.

With all of our problems in the West, we still do not have any national crisis with sufficient suffering to turn us to God as nations. However, there are millions of individuals who are facing or going through personal crises and living "quiet lives of despair."

These are the ones who are open to the church's message and are more likely to be "white unto harvest."

Only as the church understands these needs and becomes effective in ministering to and meeting these needs will we effectively communicate Christ's message of love and hope and relevance to our own nation. Only then will we be and remain a viable force in the community.

As someone else has said, "If you find a need meet it. If you find a hurt heal it." When we do this we will see much growth in the church and will never run out of business. We may not be great public speakers or great sharers of our Christian faith, but if we know how to understand and speak to people's felt needs, we can be great communicators.

As Jim Engel so aptly puts it, the key to all effective communication is to "scratch people where they itch."

To scratch people where they itch, the effective communicator obviously needs to know where they itch. That is, he must know and understand their felt needs. How to do this has been explained at the end of chapter 6—through getting to know people, by informally asking people what their needs are, by contacting schools, social and other community agencies, and through conducting formal surveys.

Questions for Study

1. Have you ever been "witnessing" to another and sensed that he was filtering out what he didn't want to hear? What did you do about it? What could you have done better?

2. When might quoting or preaching the written Word of God not be proclaiming God's message?

3. How do people process all the information that

comes to them?

4. How did Jesus get through the filter system of the people He ministered to? Give some examples of times when Jesus got people's attention by using this method.

5. What is the beginning point for all effective communication? Why is this so?

6. What is the difference between "felt needs" and "real needs"? What are some felt needs in your community? How do you perceive that you can meet the real needs by attending to the felt needs? What are some of your felt needs? List them in order of priority. Is your church ministering to these needs? Are you making your needs known to your church and Christian friends?

7. Why is it essential to begin with the listener's felt needs?

8. Can you explain the "decision process" people go through when making any major decision?

9. Do intellectual concepts alone change people's lives? Why or why not?

10. The author says that "the effective communicator will realize that he cannot change anyone," with one exception. Who is that exception? Do you agree? Why is or isn't this so?

Notes

1. James F. Engel, *What's Gone Wrong with the Harvest*, (Grand Rapids, MI: Zondervan Publishing House, 1975), pp. 25-26.

2. James F. Engel, *How Can I Get Them to Listen?* (Grand Rapids, MI: Zondervan Publishing House, 1977), p. 15.

3. Dick Innes, "Is Today's Church Boring?" *Encounter*, April 1972, p. 4.

4. James F. Engel, David T. Kollat, and Roger D. Blackwell, *Consumer Behavior*, rev. ed. (New York: Holt, Rinehart and Winston, Inc., 1973), pp. 52-54, 210-221.

5. C. Cannell and J. C. McDonald, "The Impact of Health News on Attitudes and Behavior," in *Consumer Behavior*, p. 212.

6. E. Katz, "On Reopening the Question of Selectivity in Exposure to Mass Communications," in *Consumer Behavior*, p. 212.

7. Kenneth E. Anderson, *Introduction to Communication Theory and Practice*, (Menlo Park, CA: Cummings Publishing Company, 1972), p. 46.

8. Thomas M. Steinfatt, *Readings in Human Communication*, (Indianapolis: Bobbs-Merrill Company, Inc., 1979), pp. 29-30.

9. James H. Myers and William H. Reynolds, *Consumer Behavior and Marketing Management*, (Boston: Houghton, Miflin Company, 1967), p. 134.

10. James F. Engel, *Contemporary Christian Communications*, (Nashville: Thomas Nelson, Inc., 1979), p. 117.

11. David T. Kollat, Roger D. Blackwell, and James F. Engel, *Research in Consumer Behavior* (New York: Rinehart and Winston, Inc., 1970), p. 19.

Nine

JESUS, THE COMMUNICATOR

Down the long, dusty road on their way from Jericho to Jerusalem, almost two thousand years ago, trod Jesus with His motley band of twelve disciples, followed by a huge crowd.

Because of their long journey, they were all hot and sweaty. The dust clung to them. They were weary, but Jesus was at the height of His popularity and the great crowd of people pressed close to Him. They were jabbering endlessly. Asking questions. Seeking favors. They could be heard a mile away.

"Hey, what's all the noise?" blind Bartimaeus asked his friend as they sat by the highway begging.

"I don't know," answered his friend with a puzzled tone in his voice.

"Let's ask somebody else," they agreed.

"It's Jesus," a passerby informed them.

"You mean Jesus of Nazareth, the fellow they claim can heal the sick and the blind?" Bartimaeus excitedly asked.

"That's the One," came the reply, "and I'm not going to miss seeing Him for anything. Good-bye."

The crowd came closer and closer. Excitement filled the air. The noise became intense.

"I can't believe it," shouted Bartimaeus to his friend. "This just has to be my lucky day. I've got to get to Jesus. I know He can heal me."

"Hey, Bart, there He is," cried Bartimaeus's friend, "but how will you ever get His attention?"

Dignity was dismissed. "This is it," said Bartimaeus, "I may never see Jesus again. I want to be healed."

So, seeking to drown out the noise of the crowd, Bartimaeus yelled at the top of his voice, "Jesus, have mercy on me! O Lord, son of David, have mercy on me!"

"Cool it, man! Calm down!" retorted some of the crowd to Bartimaeus. "You're making too much noise. There are so many others here you don't stand a chance of getting to Jesus, so just relax and keep quiet!"

But Bartimaeus was all the more determined to get to Jesus. He couldn't see, but he could yell. He cried out all the louder. Hear his voice rise above the din of the crowd. It rang out like a great clarion call, "Jesus, O Lord, Son of David, have mercy on me! Jesus, O Lord, Son of David, have mercy on me!"

And Jesus stood still.

And the crowds stood still.

And a great calm settled down over them all.

The winds and the waves couldn't stop the Saviour. Neither could angry mobs. Crowds of people couldn't stop Him either. But a lone, blind beggar did.

And Jesus with His great heart of compassion

asked for Bartimaeus to be brought over to Him. "What do you want me to do for you?" Jesus asked.

"Lord," Bartimaeus nervously replied, "please give me my sight."

And Jesus did. "Go your way," He said, "your faith has made you whole."

Immediately Bartimaeus could see and he followed Jesus along the way (Mark 10:46-52).

With Christ, a person's salvation usually came as a result of His having first met that person's felt need.

If Jesus had anything like a standard approach it was more likely to be a question such as the following: "What do you want me to do for you?" or "Do you want to be made whole?" or "What is your deepest need?"

The Woman at the Well

On another occasion Jesus and His disciples left Judea to head for Galilee. He wanted to go through Samaria, as He had some business to take care of on the way.

About midday Jesus was tired so He sat down and rested at Jacob's well. While His disciples were in town getting some lunch, a Samaritan woman came to draw water from the well.

I'm sure this woman was the reason for Jesus wanting to come this way. But how could He approach her? For one thing she was a Samaritan and Jesus was a Jew, and it wasn't socially or culturally acceptable for a Jew to speak to a Samaritan. She also had some personal problems which would make it look rather suspicious for Jesus to be talking to her alone. She had lived a rather colorful life and had had a few men in her time. Because of this she wasn't too popular with the other women of the town, so she came to the well alone in the middle of the day. All the other women came in the cool of the evening to draw their water.

Imagine, if you can, Jesus approaching this woman by making a statement like this: "Excuse me, lady, my name is Jesus and I'd like to ask you a personal question." And without waiting for a reply or giving her a choice He asks, "Tell me, if you should die tonight do you know where you would spend eternity?"

Not being a member of a local church she probably wouldn't have the faintest idea what He was talking about and would probably dismiss Him as being some kind of a religious freak.

But Jesus didn't approach her with any kind of a pat program. Being very sensitive to people's needs He knew that this woman was in trouble. The fact that she came to the well alone in the heat of the day was saying that. Somehow He sensed the kind of life she lived and knew that she was hurting, that underneath her brave exterior and good looks was a frightened and lonely woman. Her felt need was emotional. She needed understanding and acceptance.

Psychologists say that every life a person touches he either builds a bridge to that person or a wall between them. And Jesus, being a great bridge builder, bridged the great social gap between them by simply asking, "Please give me a drink."

This was the beginning of quite an interesting conversation. Following a brief discussion about living water, Jesus put His finger on both the need and problem area of her life. Without judging her in any way He told her that He knew she was living with a man who wasn't her husband and that she had already had five husbands.

"You have to be a prophet," she exclaimed and then turned the conversation to spiritual things herself.

She then got so excited that she left her waterpot behind, rushed back to the city and, in essence, said to the men, "Come with me. I want you to meet a man who told me all about myself with all my weaknesses and He accepted me just as I am. He didn't even criticize me. He must be the Christ." (See John 4:1-30.)

Jesus knew this woman's deepest need—her need for acceptance—and when He met it she believed in Him and automatically became a most enthusiastic witness.

Zacchaeus

Then there was Zacchaeus, the little fellow who had to climb a tree in order to see Jesus when He passed by. In spite of the great crowd of people, Jesus saw him in his tree and came over to talk to him.

I wonder just how Zacchaeus felt with Jesus looking up at him. He was a tax gatherer and, as such, was despised by the people. In a sense he was an upper-class social outcast. You can imagine some of the thoughts and feelings racing through his mind: "I wonder what Jesus is going to say to me? I'm scared to death. Will he condemn me too?"

But his fears were quickly allayed. Sensing Zacchaeus's deep social need and a need for a friend, Jesus quietly said, "Come down, my friend, I would like to go home with you for dinner tonight."

When Jesus met his felt need, Zacchaeus, of his own initiative, confessed his sin and promised to make restitution to all he had cheated (Luke 19:1-10).

The Man at Bethesda

In Jerusalem there was a pool called Bethesda where many sick, crippled, blind, and impotent people waited. This particular pool was visited from time to time by an angel after which it had certain healing powers for the first person who entered the water.

One of those many people lying on his bed beside the pool was a man who had been crippled for thirty-eight years! One day Jesus came to him and said, "Would you like to be made whole?"

The impotent man replied pathetically, "But, sir, I don't have anybody to put me in the pool when the waters are visited. And while I am struggling to get there, somebody else always beats me."

Then Jesus said to him, "Rise, take up your bed, and walk."

And the man did. Jesus had healed him—and left without even telling the man who He was or why He healed him.

It was at a later point of time that Jesus spoke to this man about spiritual matters (John 5:1-15). The man's need was obviously physical and Jesus met him at that point of need first.

Rebecca Pippert explains how Jesus "had an extraordinary ability to see beneath the myriad of layers of people and know what they longed for, or really believed, but were afraid of revealing. That is why His answers so frequently did not correspond to the questions He was asked. He sensed their unspoken need or question and responded to that instead. Jesus could have healed lepers in countless ways. To the leper in Mark 1:40-45 He could have shouted, 'Be healed . . . but don't get too close. I just hate the sight of lepers.' He didn't. Jesus reached over and touched him. Jesus' touch was not necessary for his physical healing. It was critical for his emotional healing.

"Can you imagine what it meant to that man to be touched? A leper was an outcast, quite accustomed to walking down a street and seeing people scatter, shrieking at him, 'Unclean—unclean!' Jesus knew that this man not only had a diseased body but an equally diseased self-concept. He needed to be touched to be fully cured. And so Jesus responded as He always did, with total healing for the whole person."[1]

The Woman Caught in Adultery

Perhaps one of the most beautiful examples of communicating Christ's love in the entire New Testament is where Christ ministered to the woman who was caught in the act of adultery.

Why the scribes and Pharisees brought only the woman to Jesus for judgment is a little difficult to understand. How a woman could be caught in the act of adultery alone is beyond my comprehension. If the truth could be known, the guilty man may very well have been one of the accusers. If I were a betting man, I'd bet he was. The whole affair was undoubtedly a setup to trap Jesus. Not only was this woman being used, but terribly abused.

Regardless, you can just see these religious bigots gloating over their victory. "We've got Him cornered at last," they bragged among themselves with a false sense of anticipated triumph. "He can't win. And we can't lose. Whatever way He answers, He's damned. If He says to punish her according to the law of God, we'll accuse Him of having no mercy. If He says to let her go free, we'll accuse Him of breaking God's law."

So there they stood around Jesus and the guilty woman. They were like a pack of hungry dogs just waiting for the signal to pounce on Jesus and devour Him.

What did they care about the woman? Absolutely nothing. They were using her as a pawn in their game.

"Now, Master," they sarcastically addressed Jesus, "this woman was caught committing adultery—in the very act. God's law demands that such a woman be stoned to death. How do you feel about that? What's your judgment?"

Jesus ignored them. He stooped down and wrote on the ground. But these men were persistent. They were determined to win their devious game so they kept pressing Jesus for an answer.

So Jesus stood up, looked at them, and agreed with them. "Yes," he said, "you're absolutely correct. The law of Moses, God's law, does say that such a woman should be stoned to death."

"He's agreeing with us," they mused among themselves, and you could see them going for the rocks tucked under their religious robes—the rocks of accusation they were about to hurl at Jesus. They were more concerned about killing Jesus than they were about stoning the woman or defending justice.

"So," continued Jesus, "go ahead and stone her to death if that's what you desire."

After a brief moment's pause and with a burning look that pierced the depths of their consciences Jesus added, "However, gentlemen, wait just a minute, I'd like to add one condition—let the man who has never sinned cast the first stone."

Thud.

Their own accusations had boomeranged on themselves. They weren't prepared for that answer. The silence was deafening. And now like frightened puppy dogs, they tucked their "religious" tails between their legs and got out of there as quickly as they could.

Jesus was left alone with the woman. He knew she'd been used. He understood her deepest need and gently asked her, "What happened to your accusers? Where did they go? Isn't there anyone left to condemn you?"

"No, Lord," she replied, "they've all gone."

Then Jesus made a simple but profound statement: "I don't condemn you either. Go, and don't commit this sin anymore." (See John 8:1-11.)

The crucial issue to see and understand in this situation was not that Jesus won, nor was it that the woman was set free. The profound dynamic in communicating His message in this story was this: Before Jesus told this woman to go and sin no more He first met the basic need in her life, the lack of which was causing her to sin.

This is such a profound truth, it desperately needs understanding. Let me explain. Counselors tell us that a prostitute, for example, is a woman who has been hurt deeply by her father—perhaps by her mother too, but mostly by her father. She is very hostile towards him. He didn't meet her needs for love, acceptance, and approval. Neither did he confirm her womanhood. For one or many reasons she felt rejected by him. She doesn't come to this conclusion consciously, but the greatest way she can get back at her father is by becoming a prostitute. She is also desperately searching for the father's love she never received as a child or as a young woman and is unconsciously trying to prove to herself that she is a woman. She is being driven into acts of sin because of unresolved hurt, anger and by an unmet need for love and acceptance.

The same principle applies to the man who is running around using women. His problem includes lust, but it goes far deeper. He is not the great masculine figure he thinks he is. He may be angry at his mother and be using other women as a means of expressing his hostility. Or he may be still searching for the mother's love and acceptance he never received as a child as well as trying to convince himself that he is adequate as a male.

Behind all external acts of sin, there is almost always a deeper sin, fault, unmet need, or damaged emotion. In other words, all behavior is caused or motivated. There is a reason why people do what they do. This is not to excuse their behavior. Not at all. Jesus didn't condemn the woman for her sin, but neither did He condone her actions. He told her not to do it again. However, He knew that this woman had a deep emotional need in her life and it was this unmet need that was driving her into acts of sin.

In meeting her needs, Jesus could realistically say to her, "Go and don't commit this sin anymore."

We tend to see sin as only the external act. But this external act is merely the tip of the iceberg. Sin is anything that falls short of the perfection God planned for us. It includes all of our damaged emotions, our wounded personality, our mixed motives, our unresolved inner conflicts, and our supercharged repressed negative emotions. These are the pains that keep us in bondage to ourselves and cause us to act out in sinful ways. These are the barriers that alienate us from God, from others, and from our-